nail artistry

Everyday Nail Art

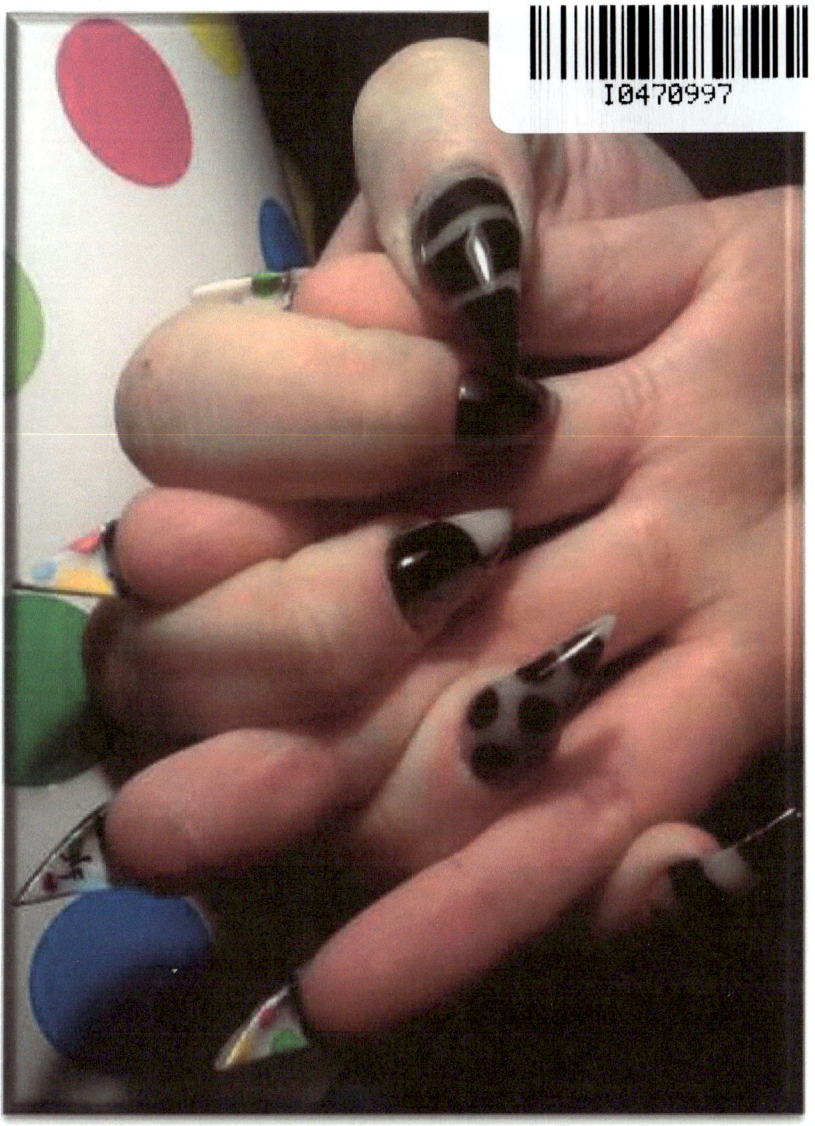

Author: melinda nailfanatic

ISBN-13: 978-1482005066
ISBN-10: 1482005069

DEDICATION

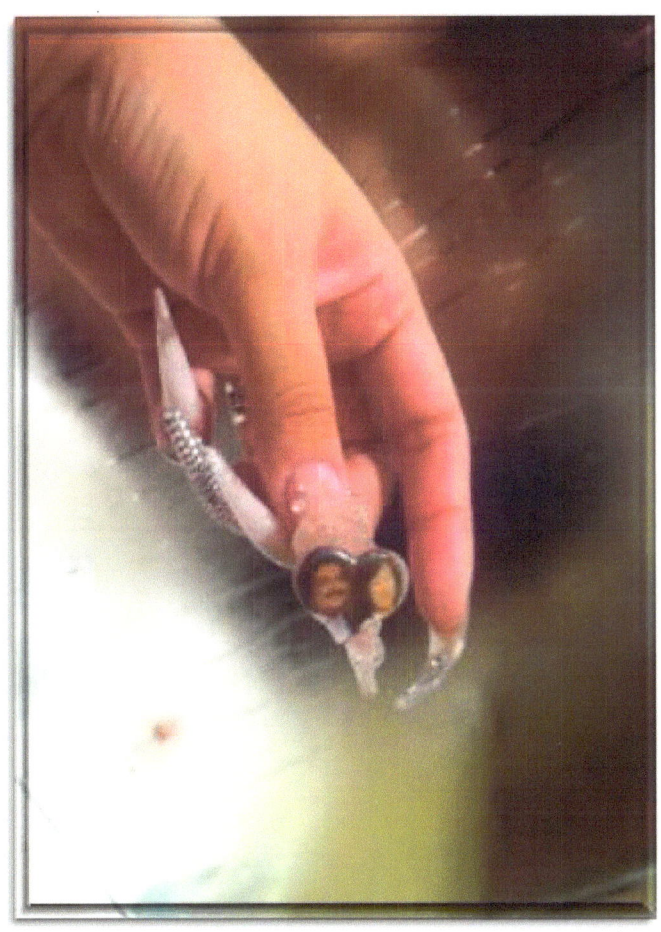

SPECIAL THANKS

My amazing, intelligent, bold, confident, inspired, unique, original, creative, fun-loving, happiness sharing powerfully divine family definitely deserves a wonderful heartfelt "Thank you. Thank you! THANK YOU!"

All Nail Fanatics© past, present and future who wear these nails every day. You are the reason that this is the wildflower of a creation it is, it will always continue to grow and grow.

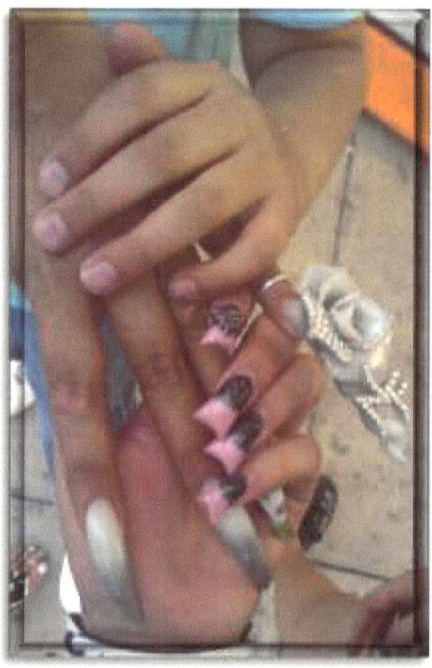

ACKNOWLEDGMENTS

I am so grateful to the many amazing people who have been there with me so far whether they have come to stay, or only come to stay for a period of time and bless us with understanding in the wake of their leave. Life is definitely a journey and the inspiration for these works of art come as an embellishment to the journey. The journey is made more interesting and beautiful by the divine personalities that we encounter who come into our lives as earth angels to bless us, each in their own way. So to all those who choose to be a part of my journey, I am ever grateful to you and I thank you for walking and talking with me on this my life's journey.

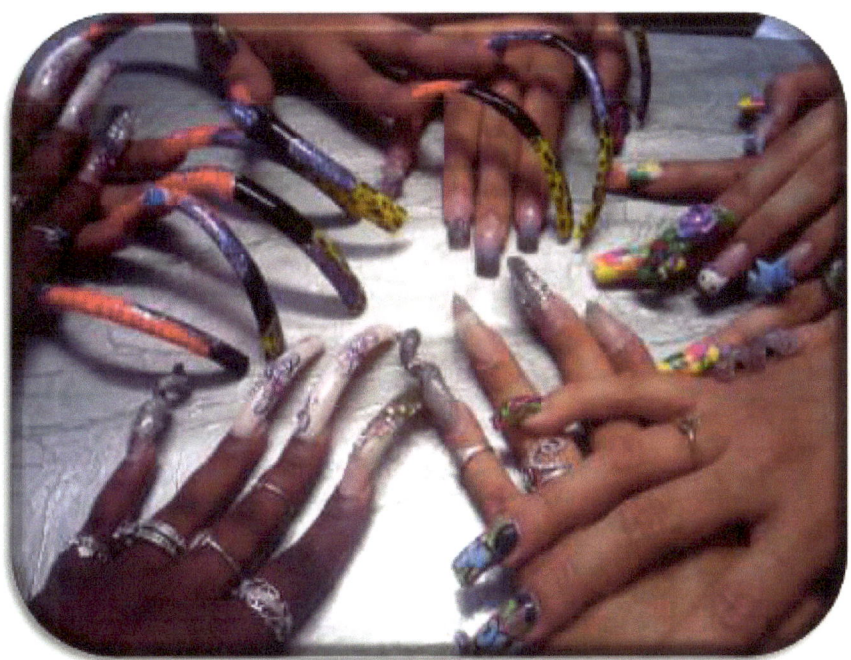

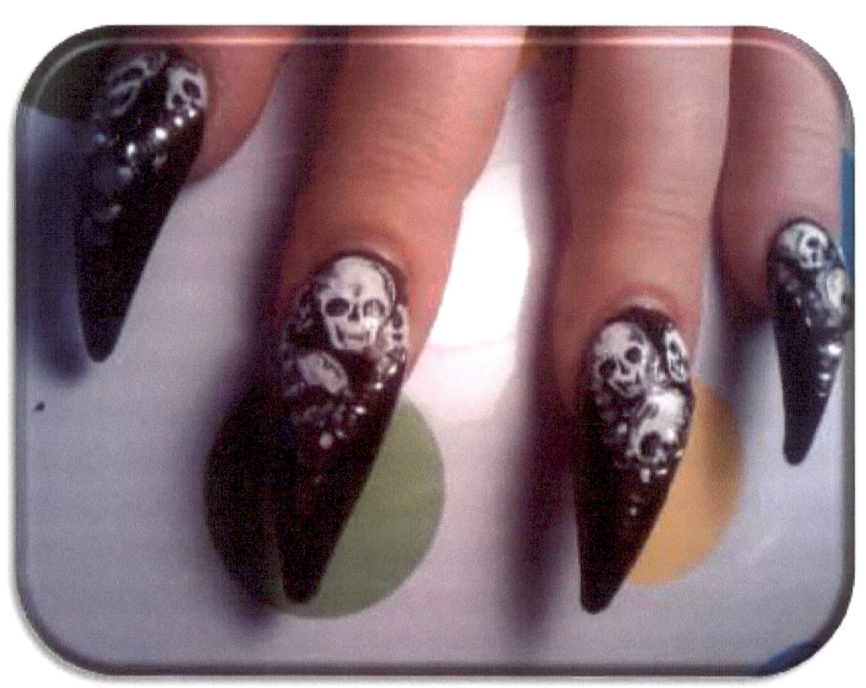

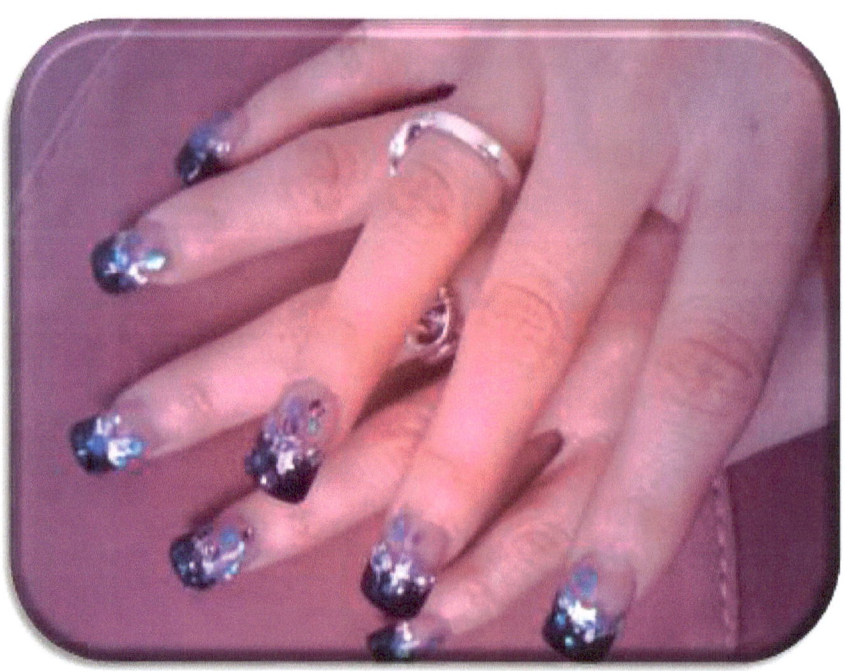

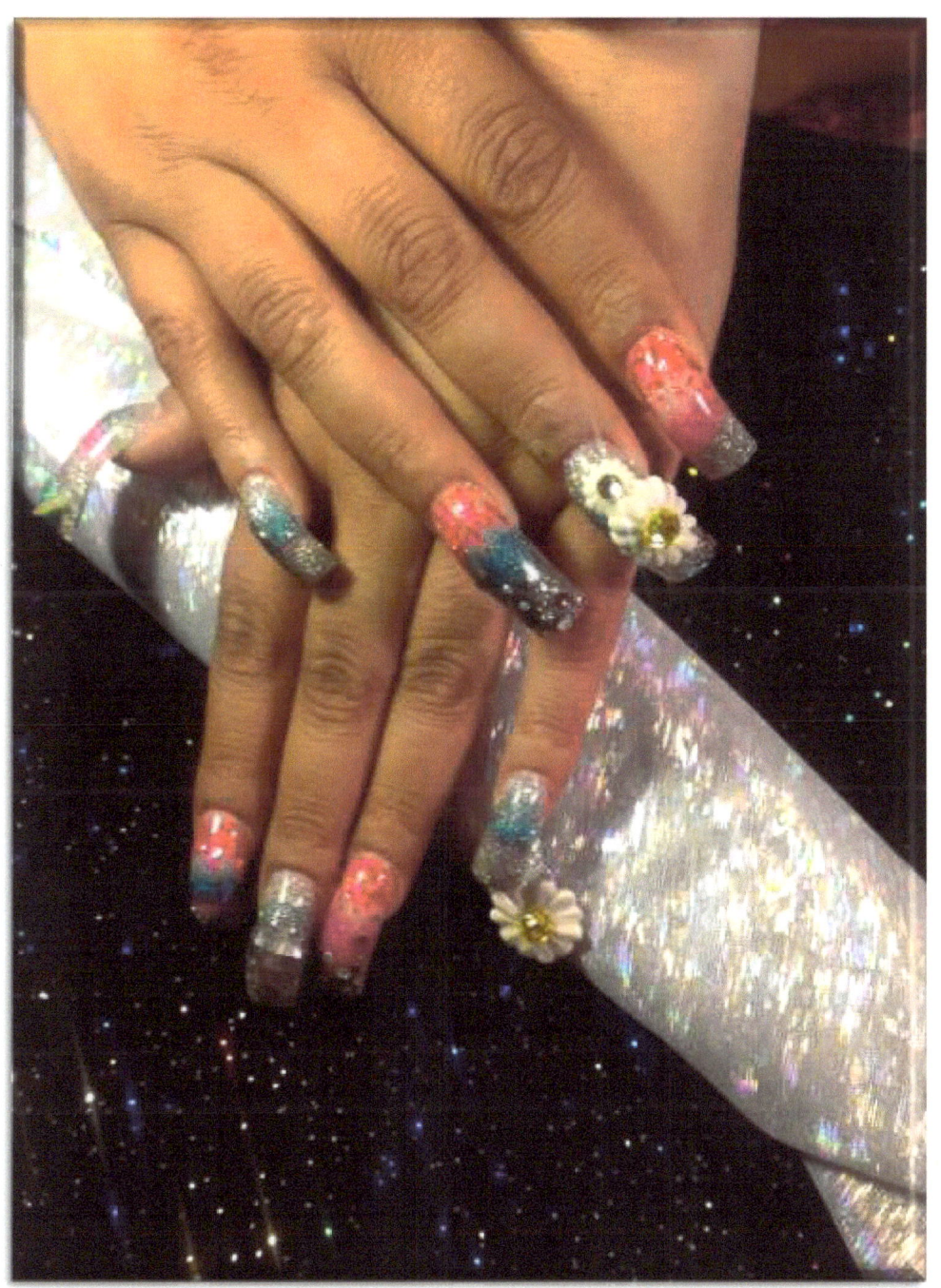

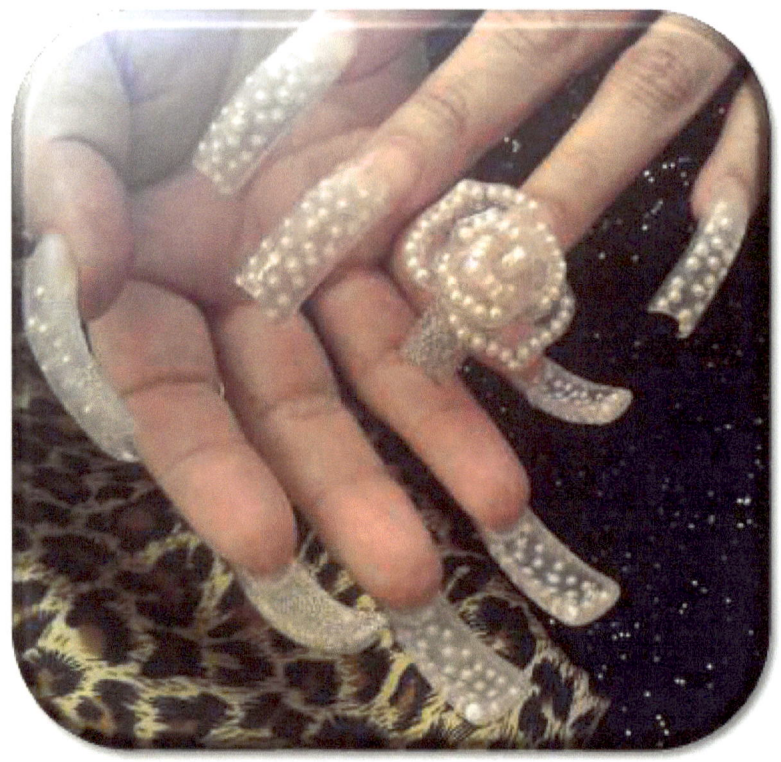

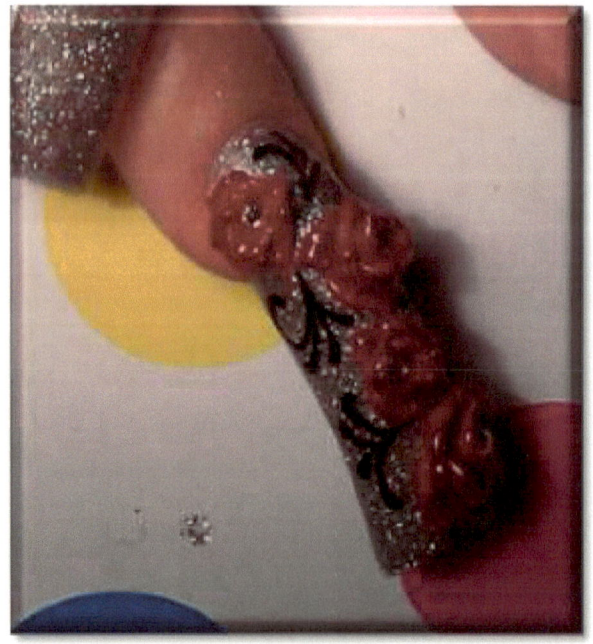

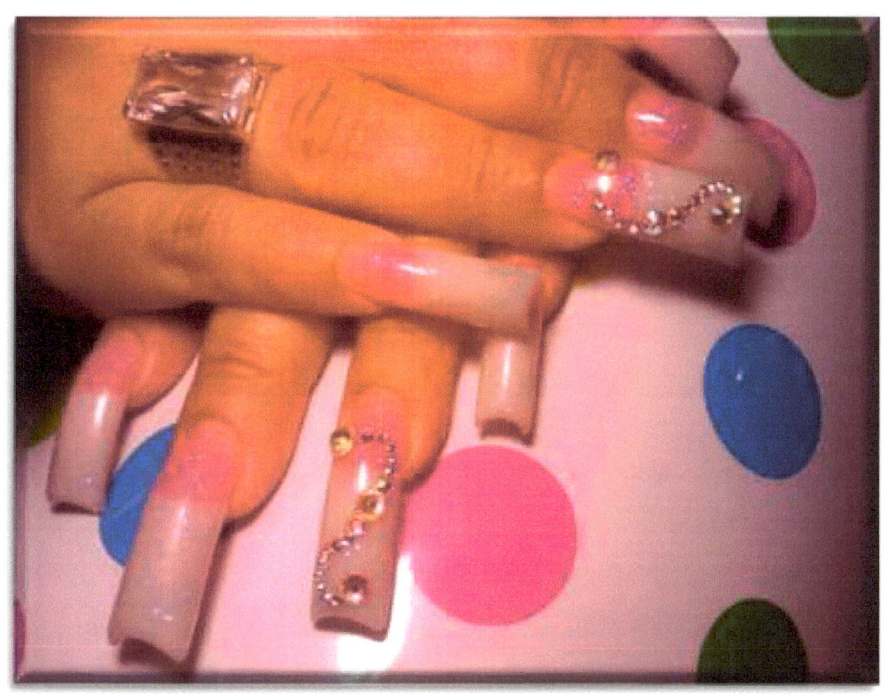

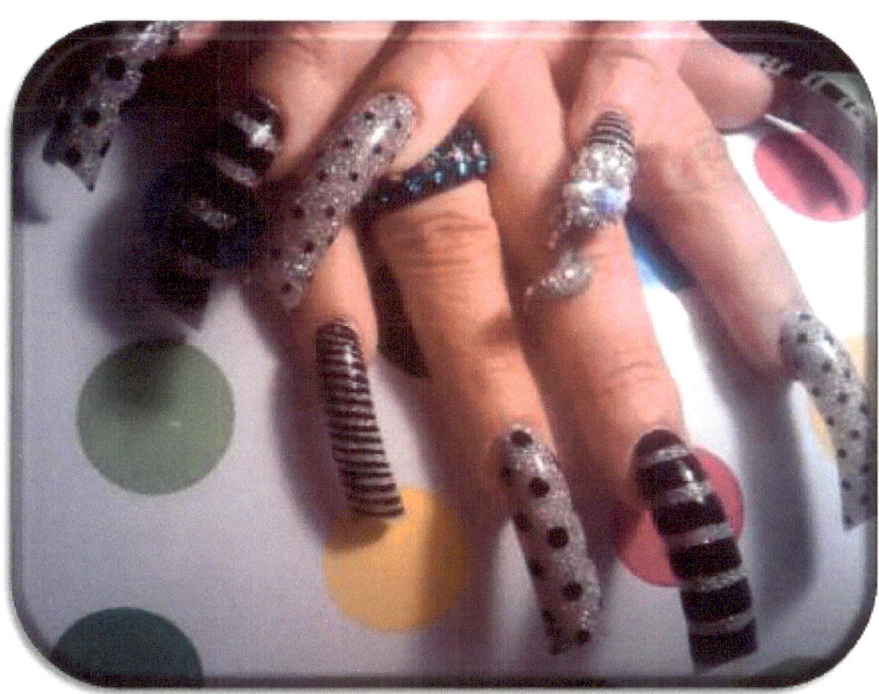

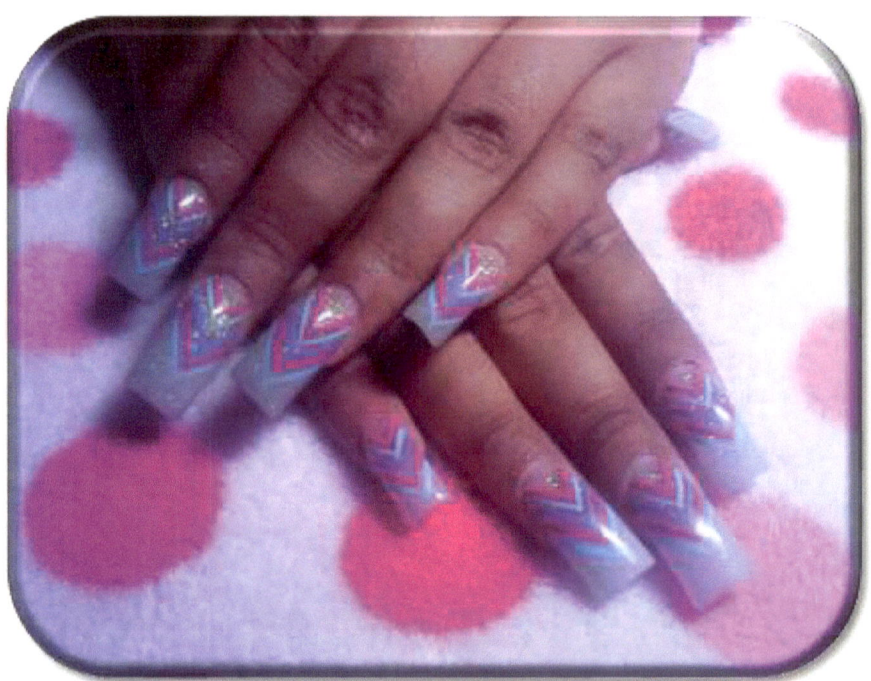

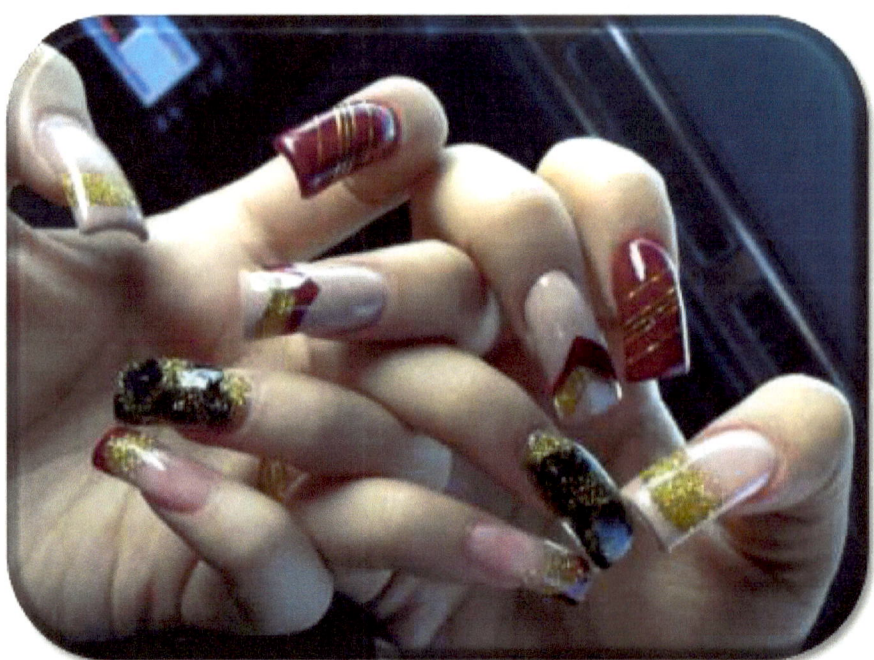

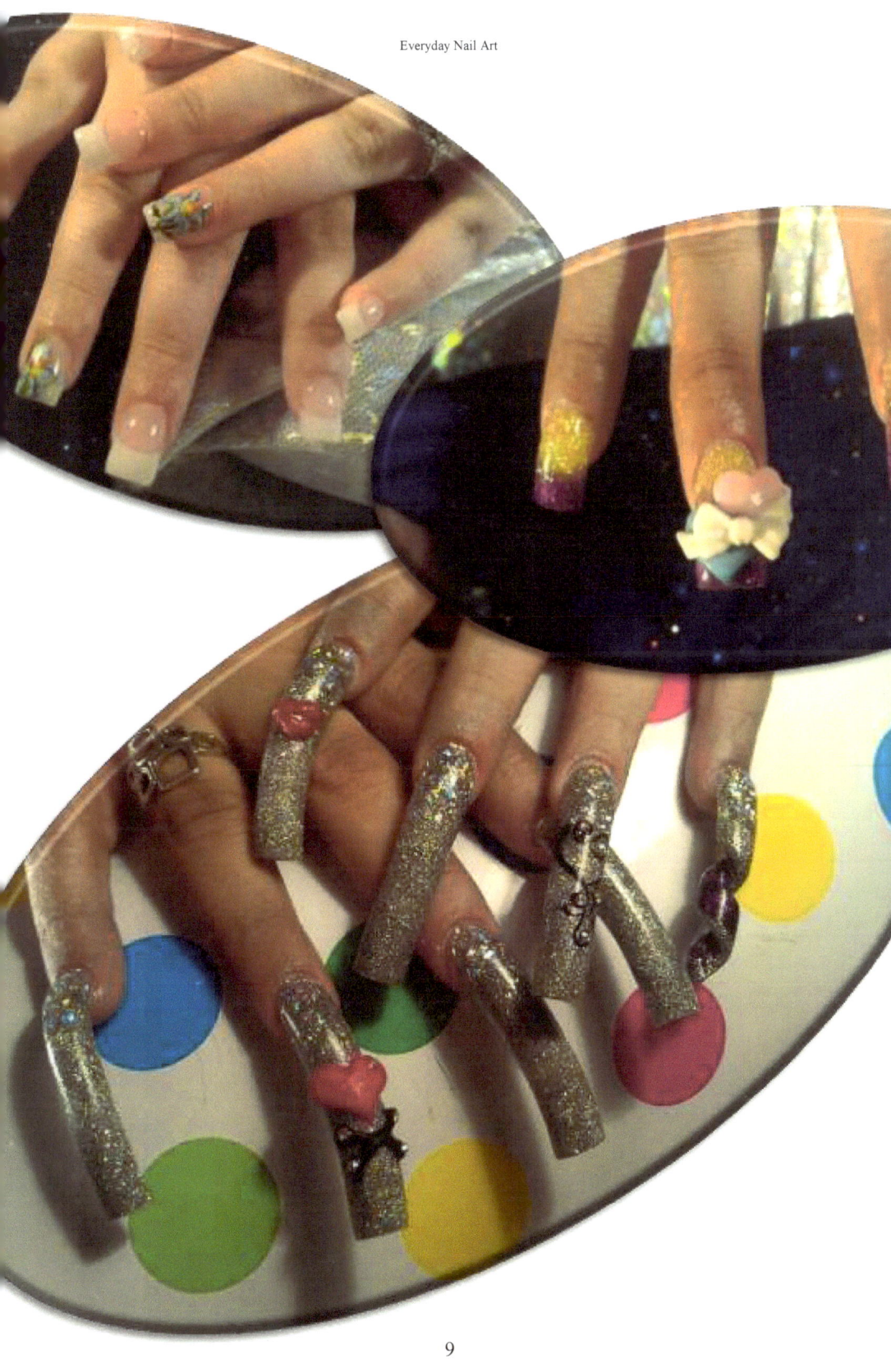

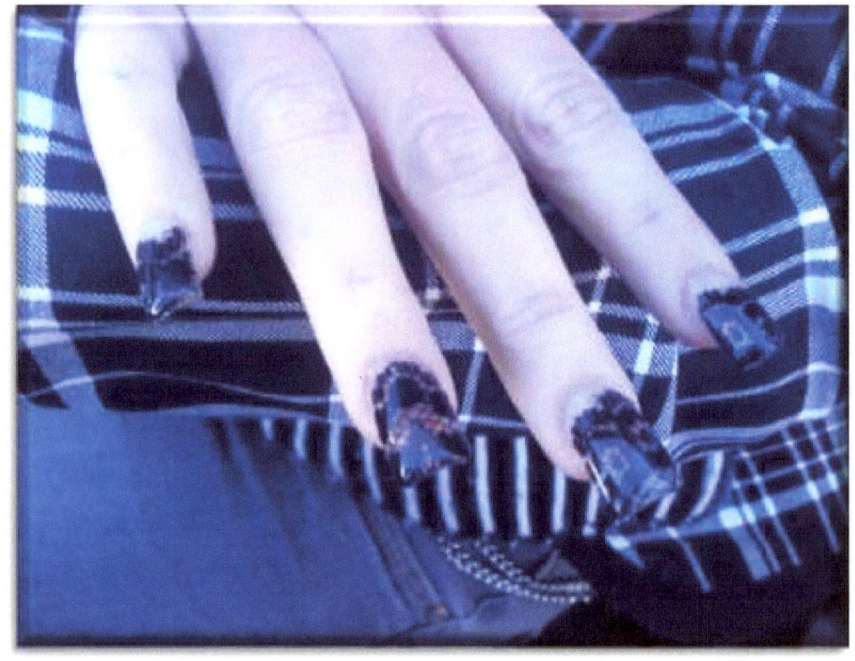

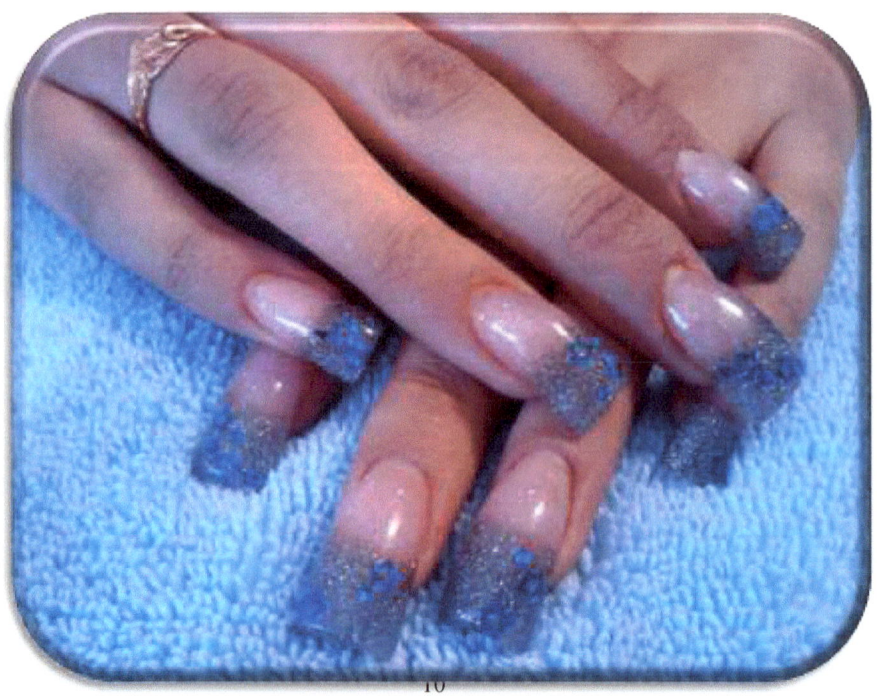

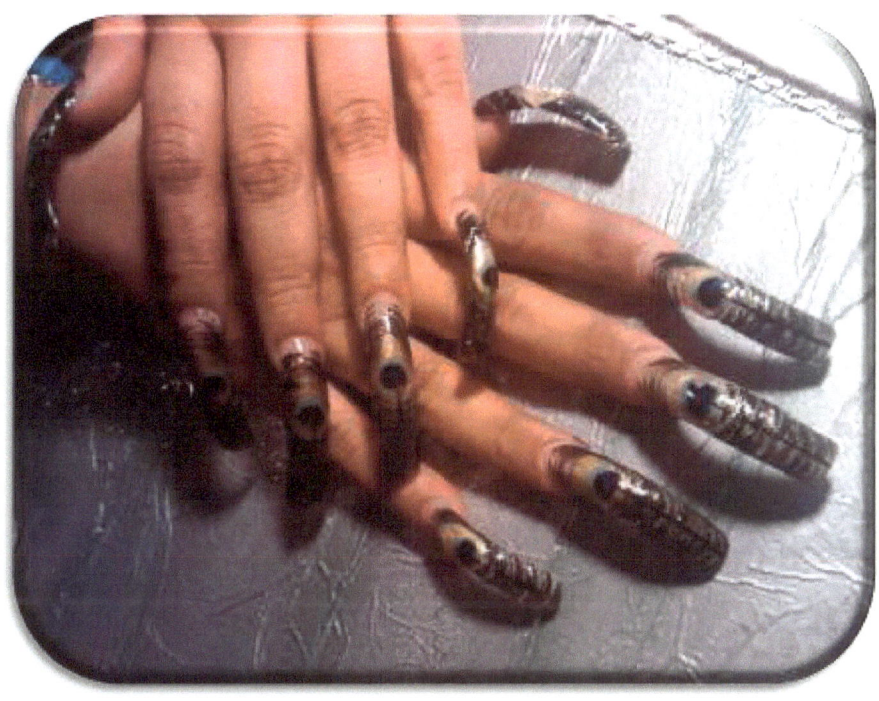

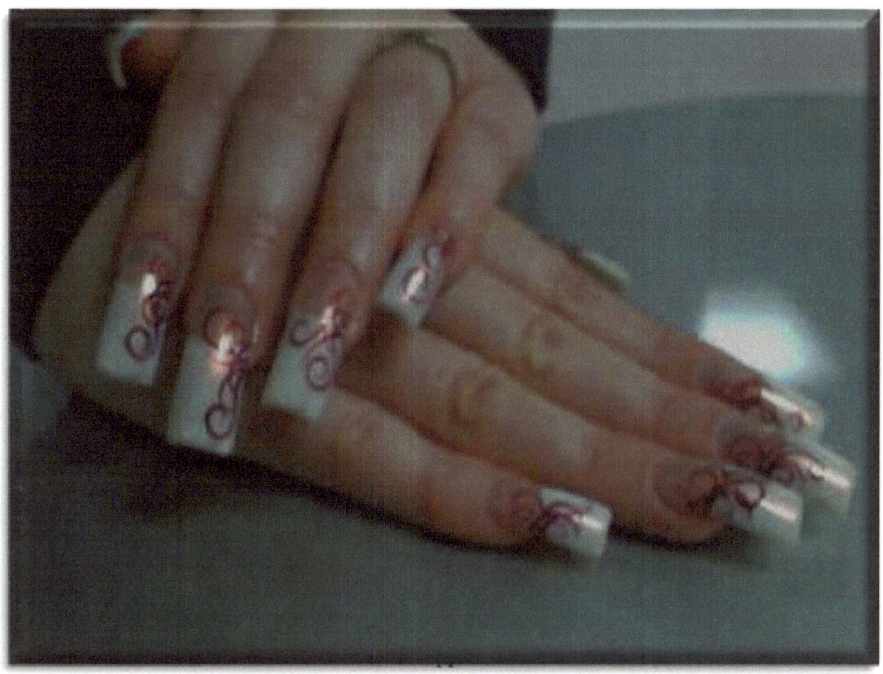

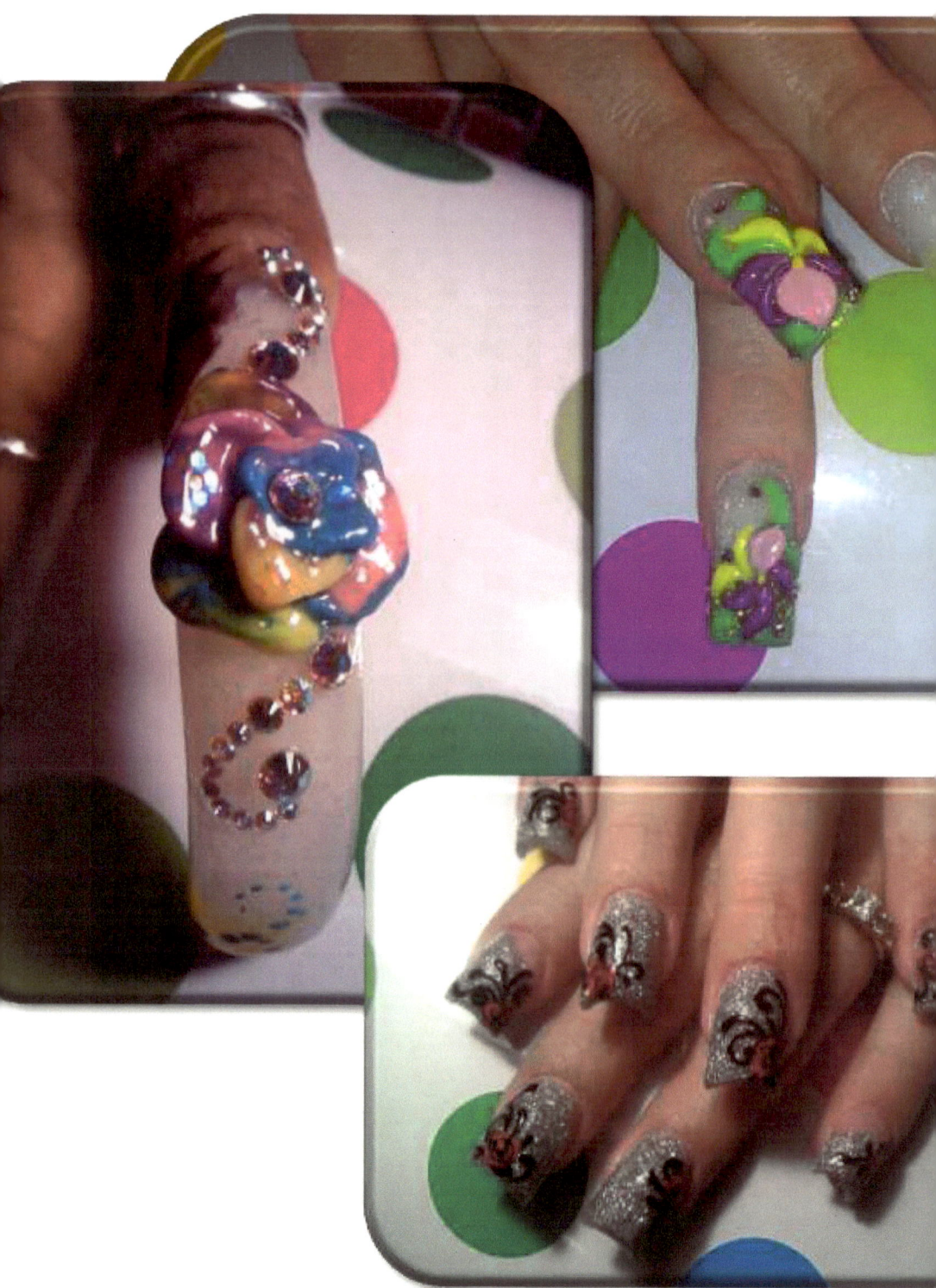

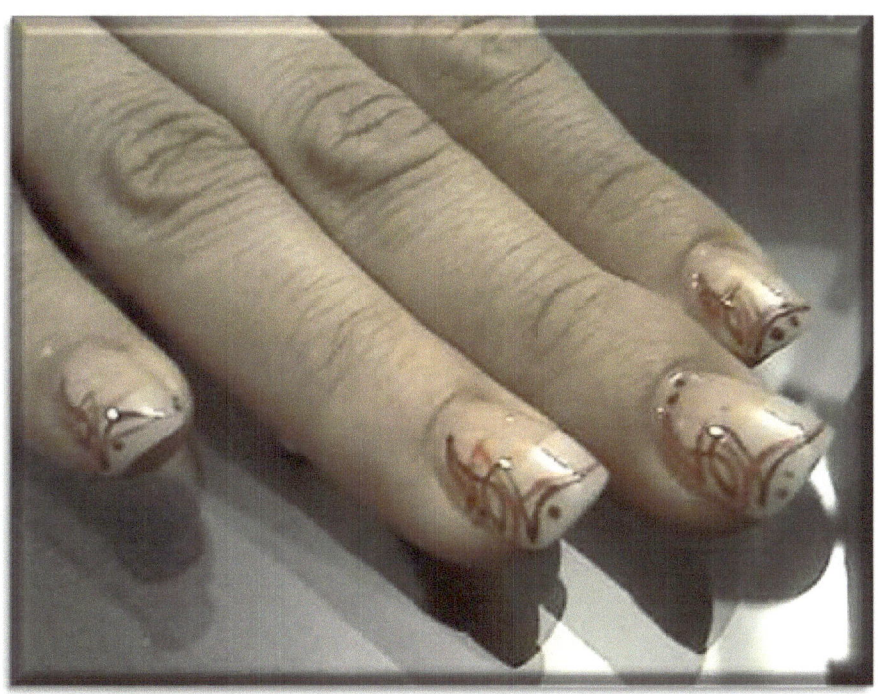

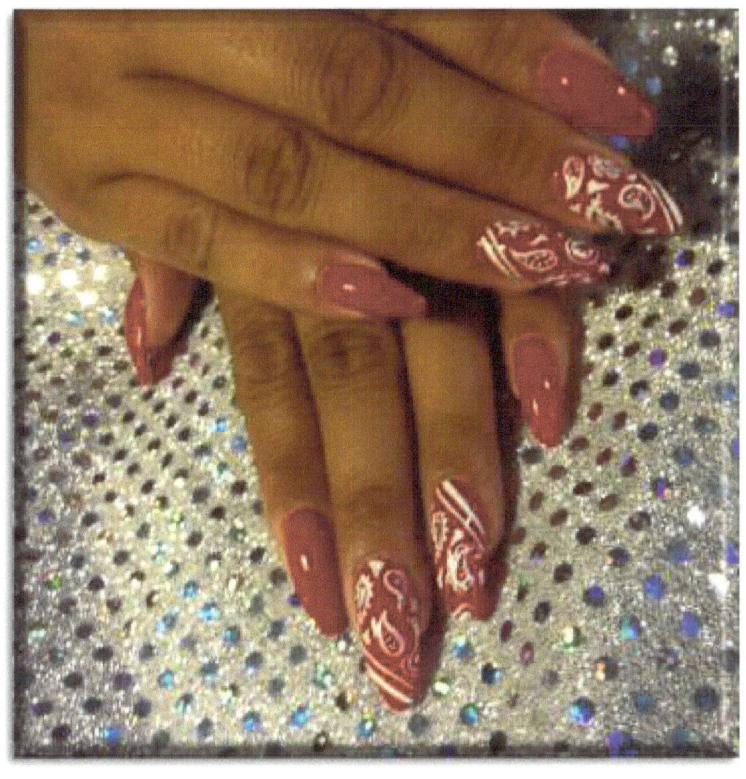

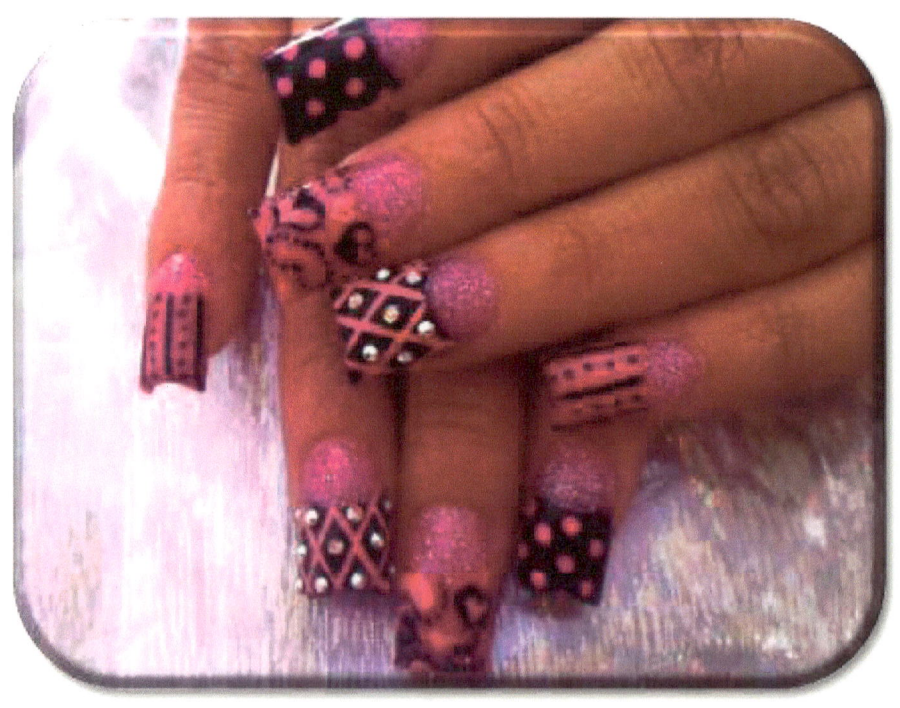

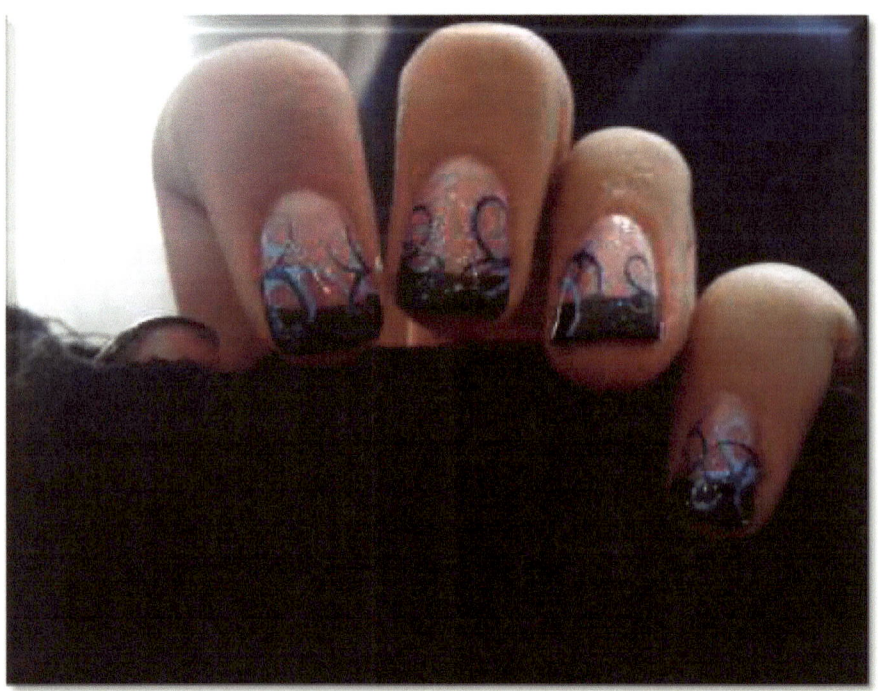

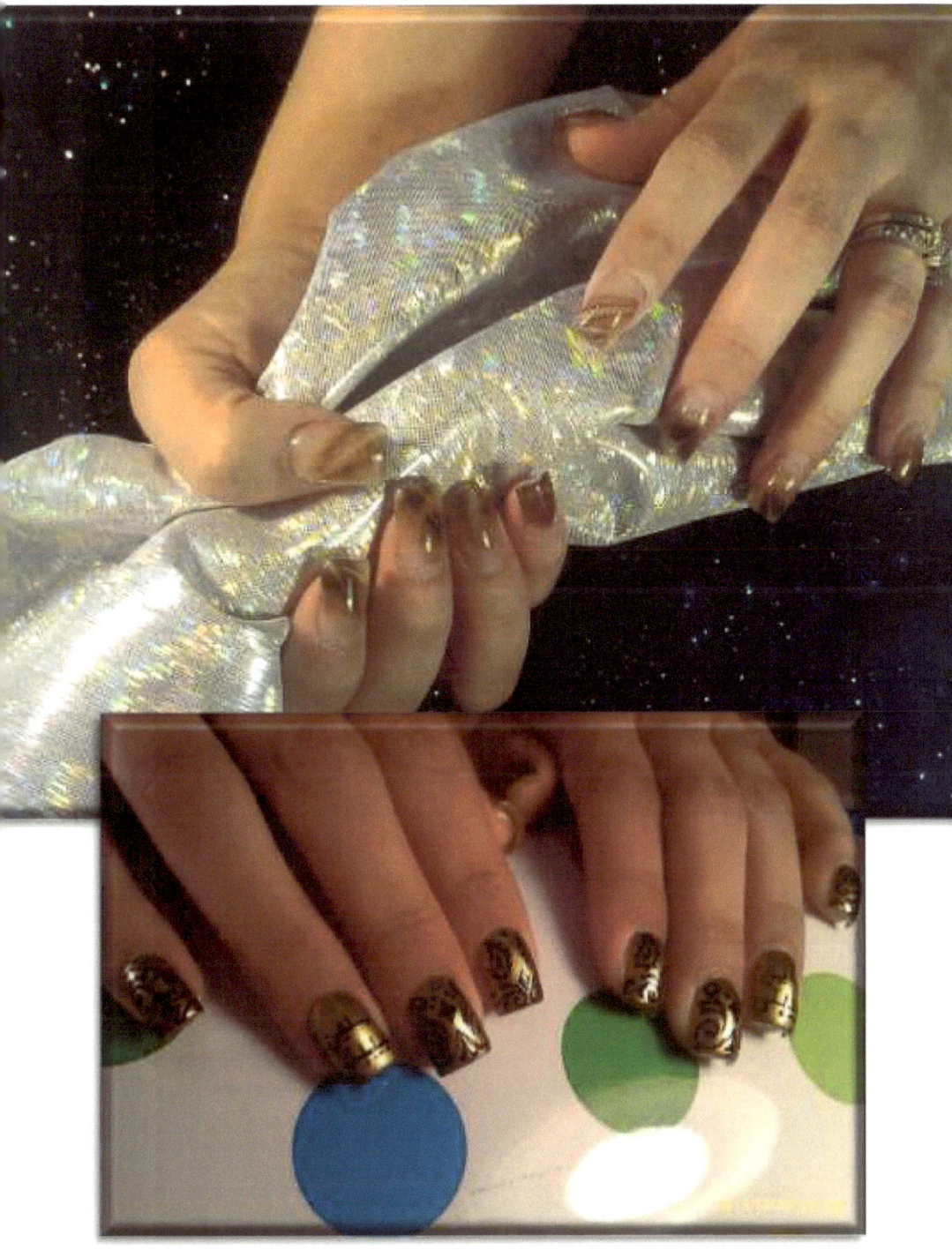

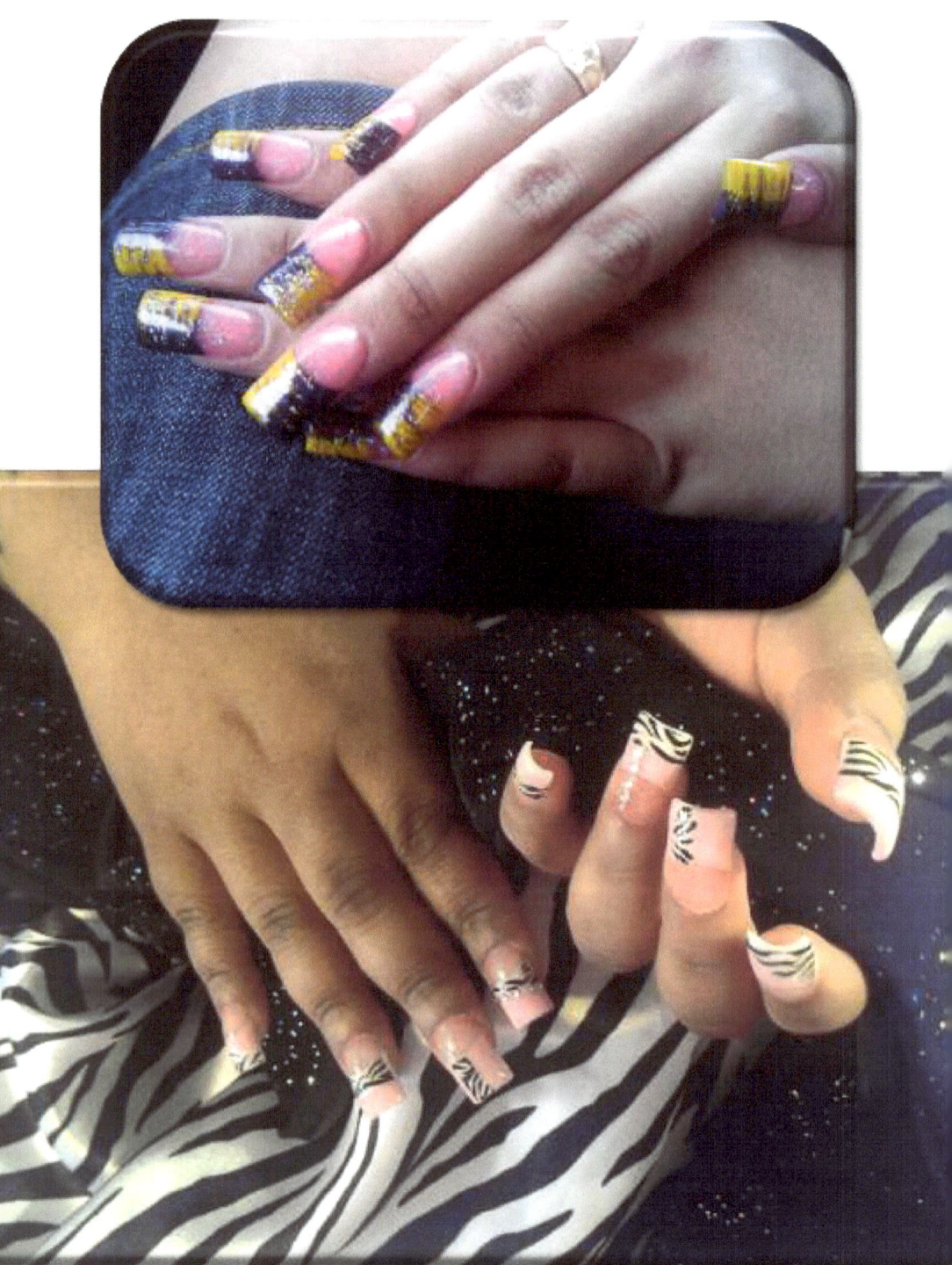

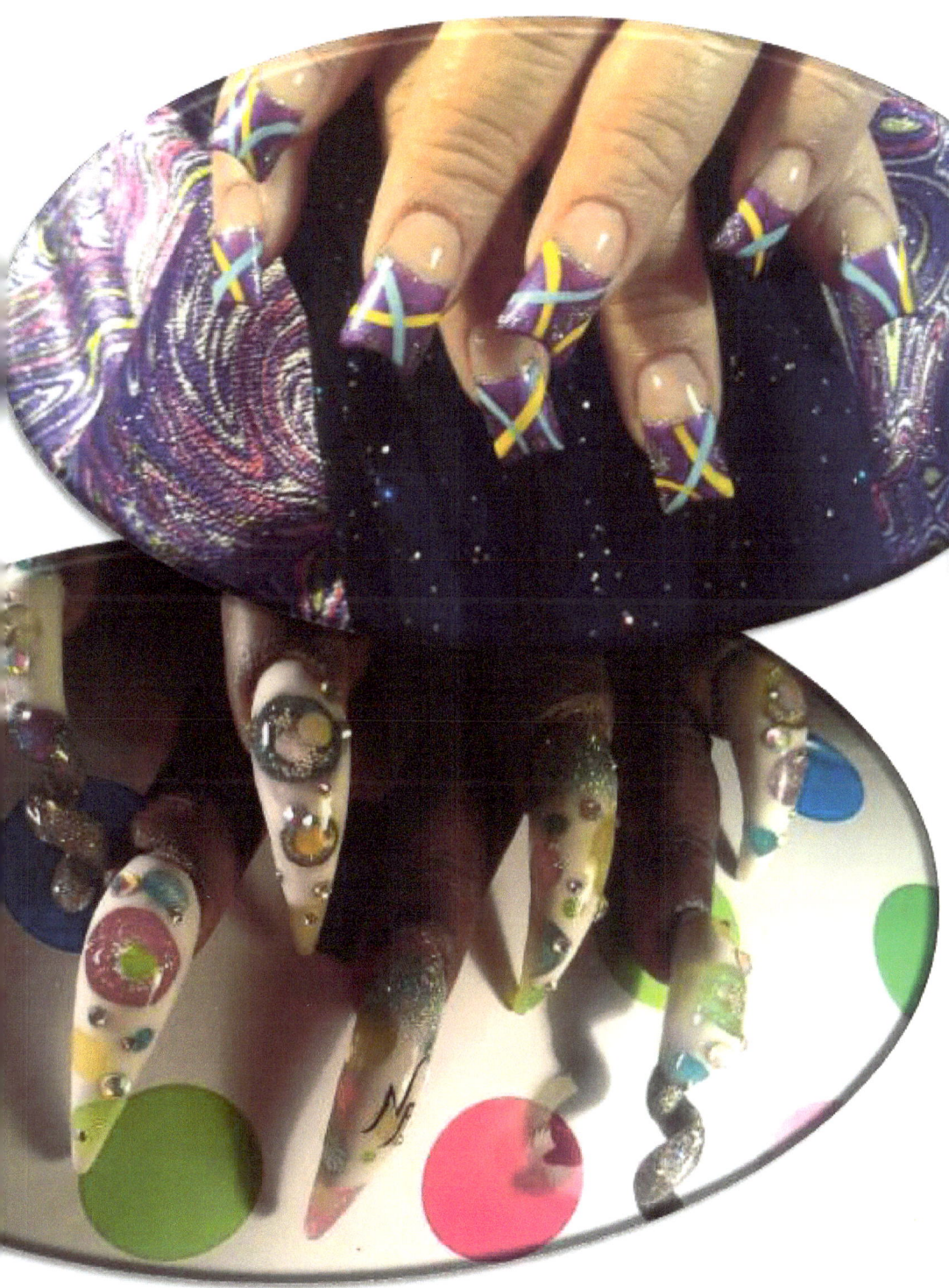

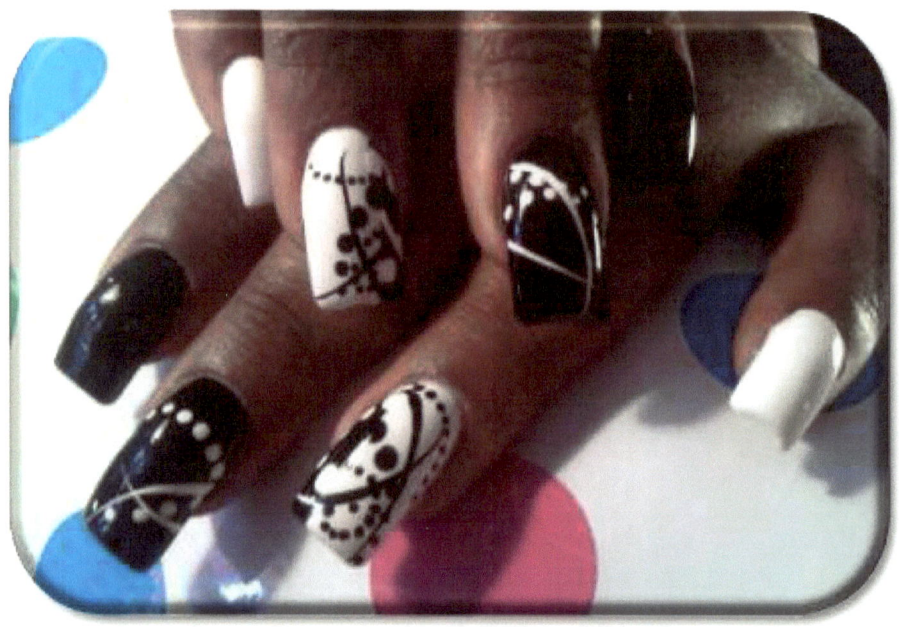

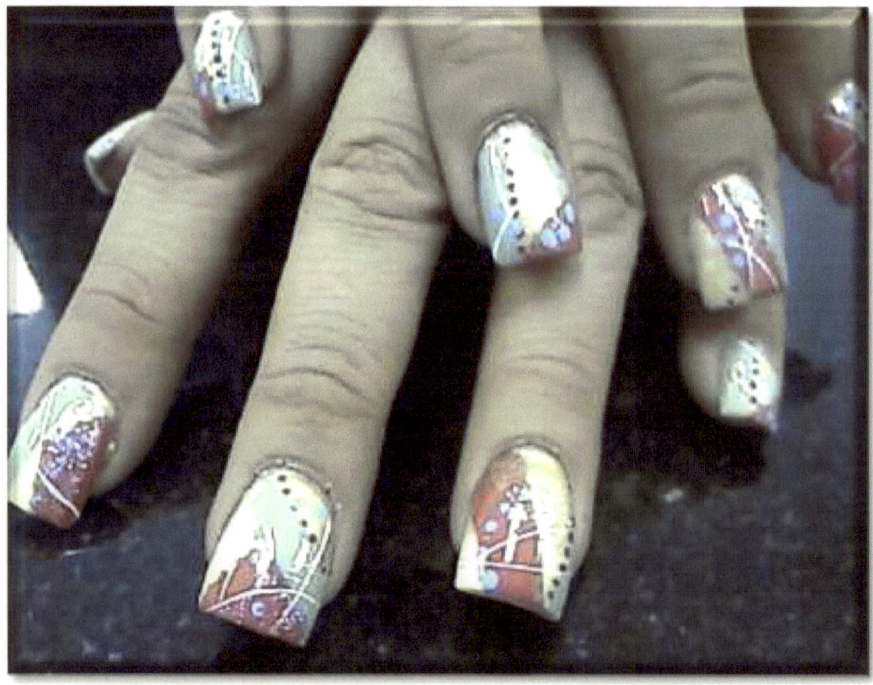

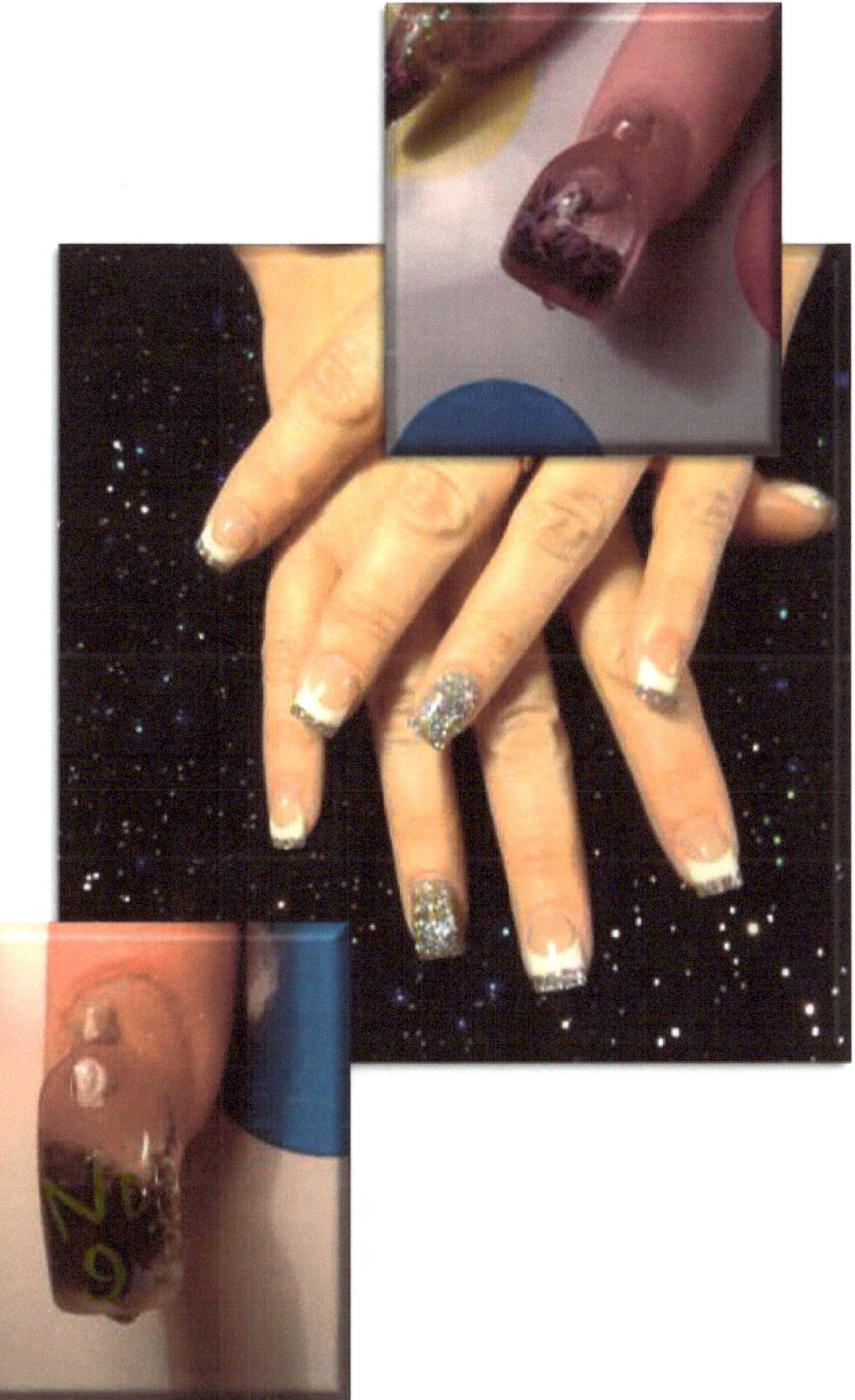

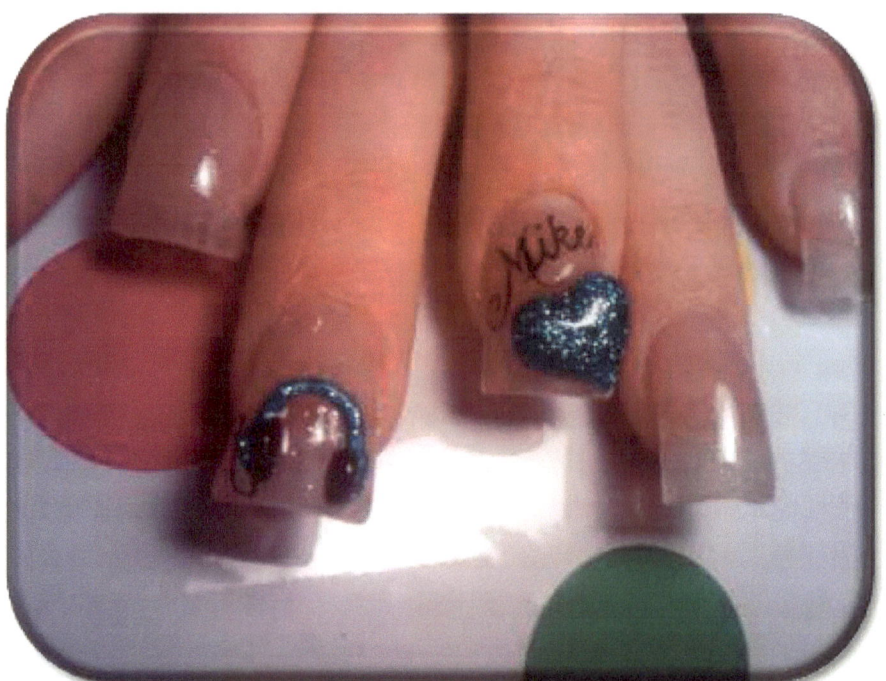

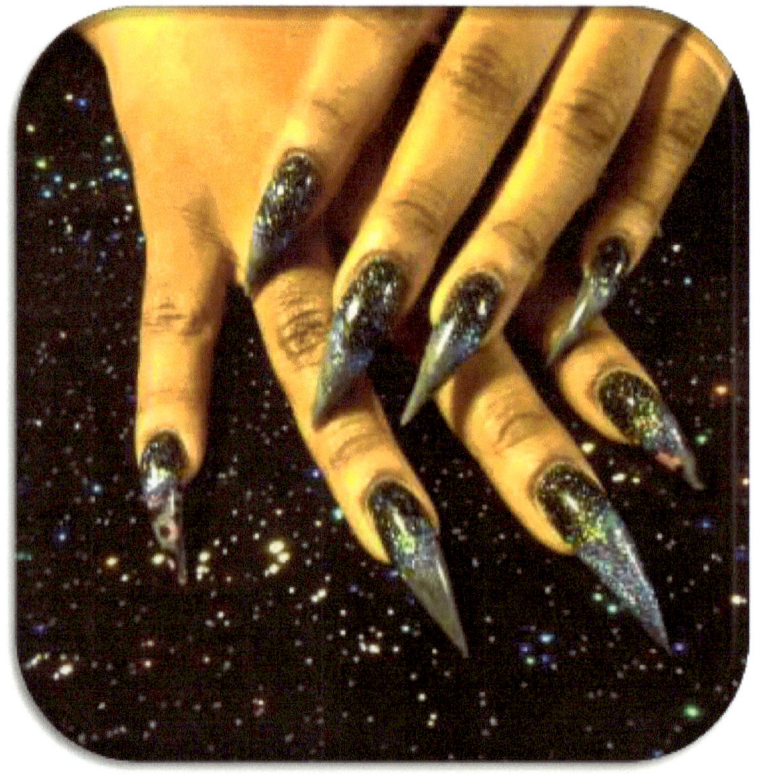

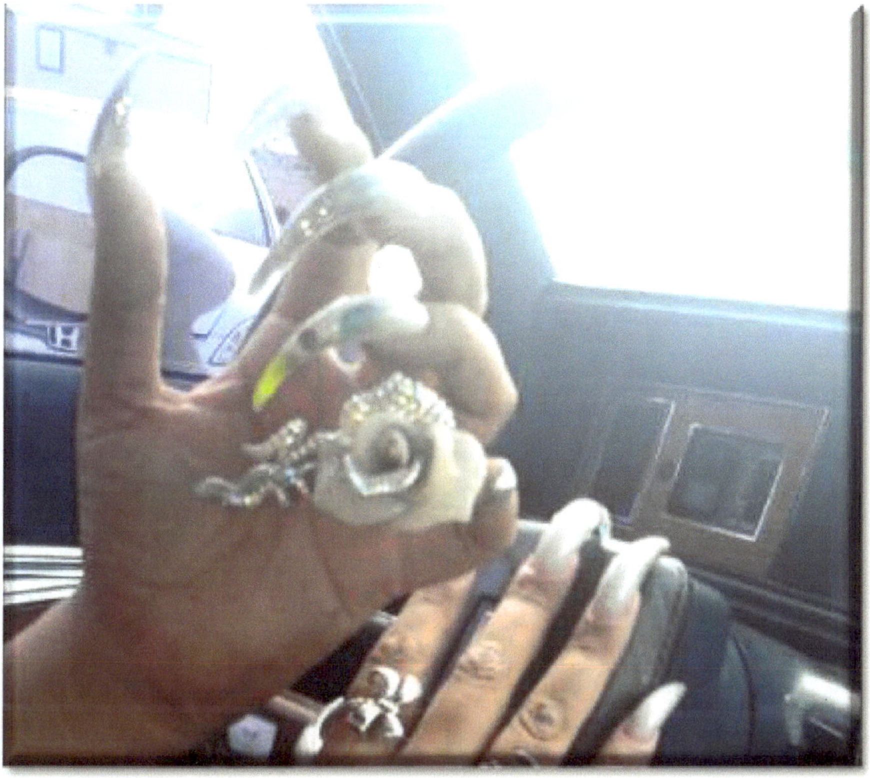

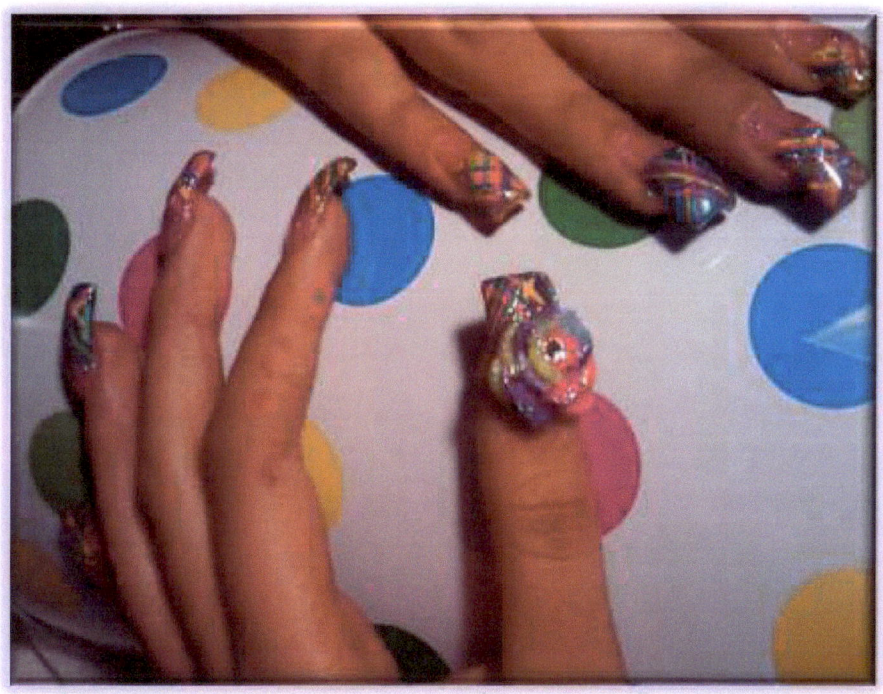

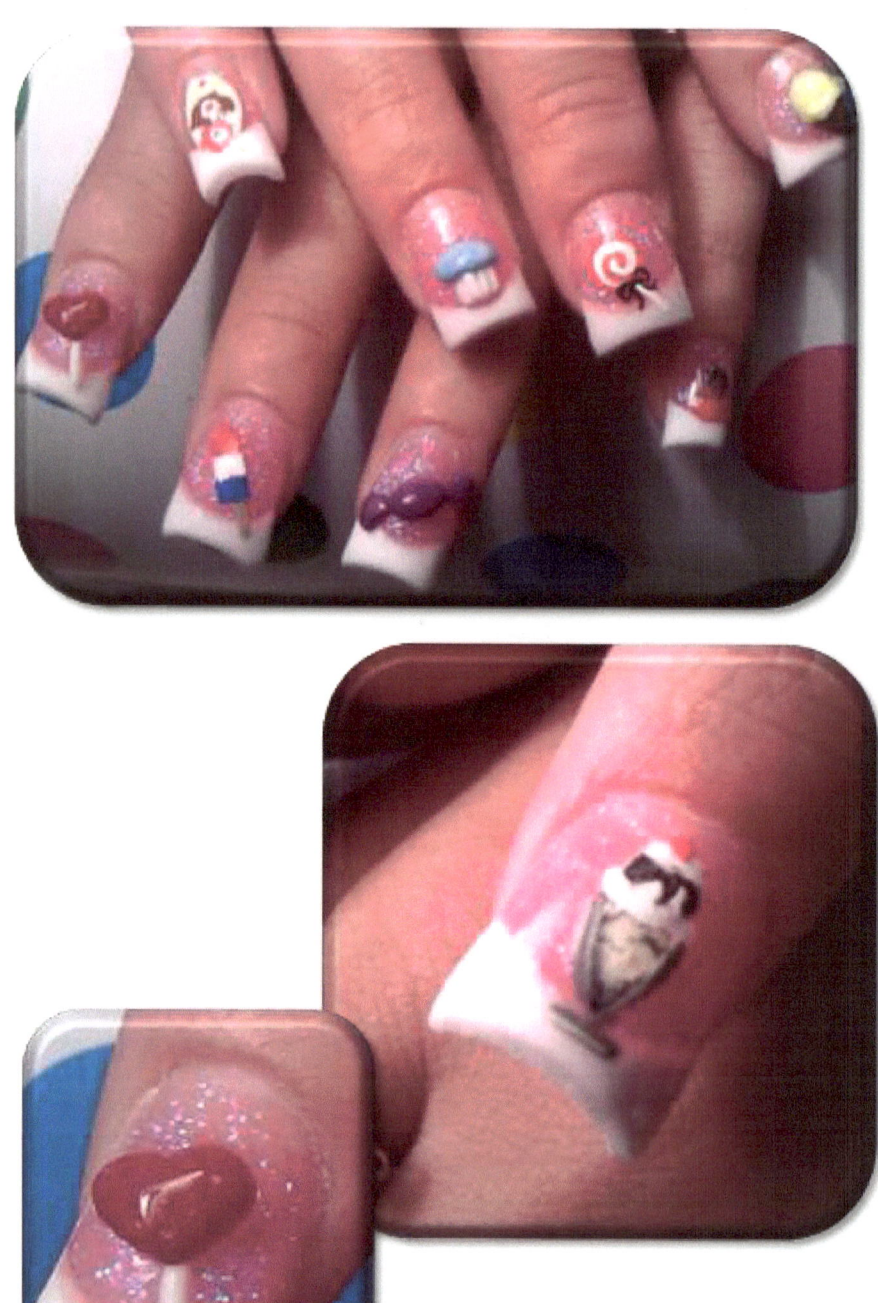

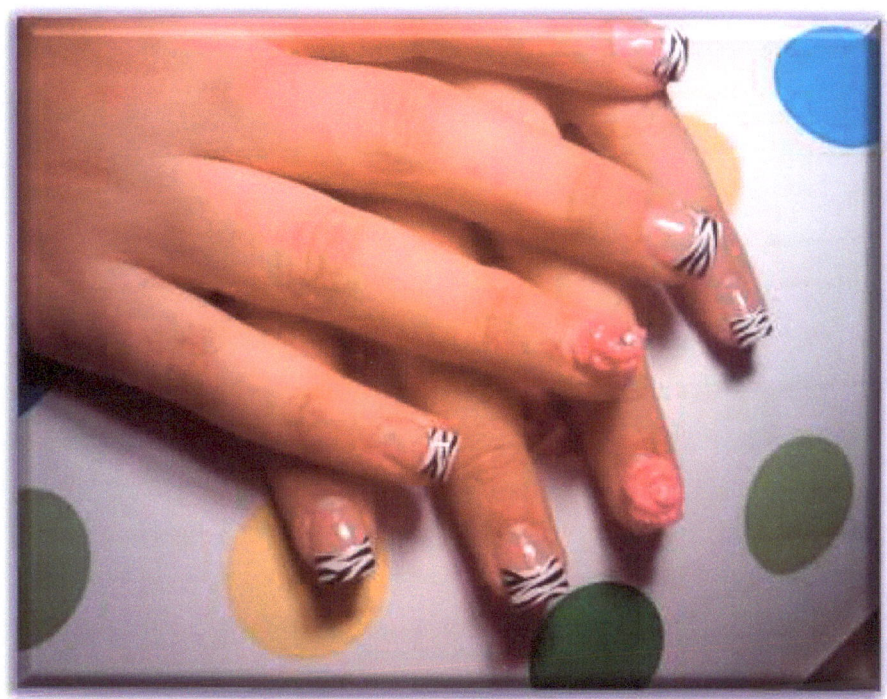

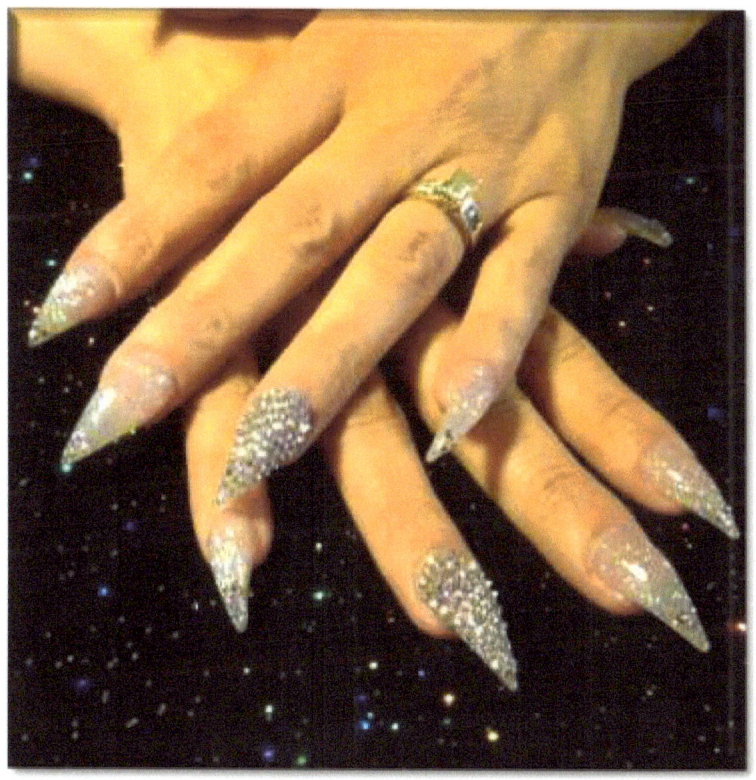

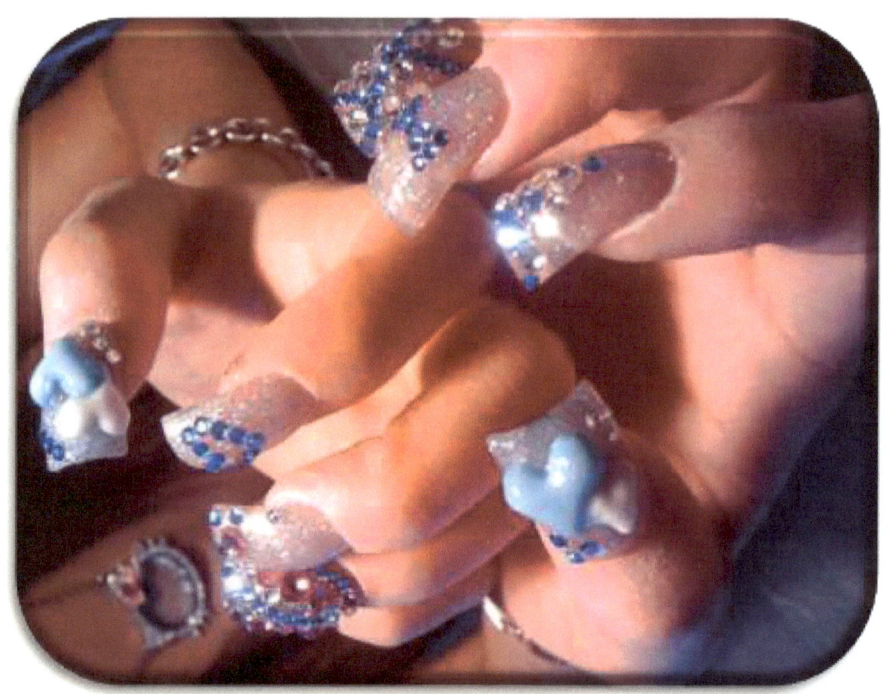

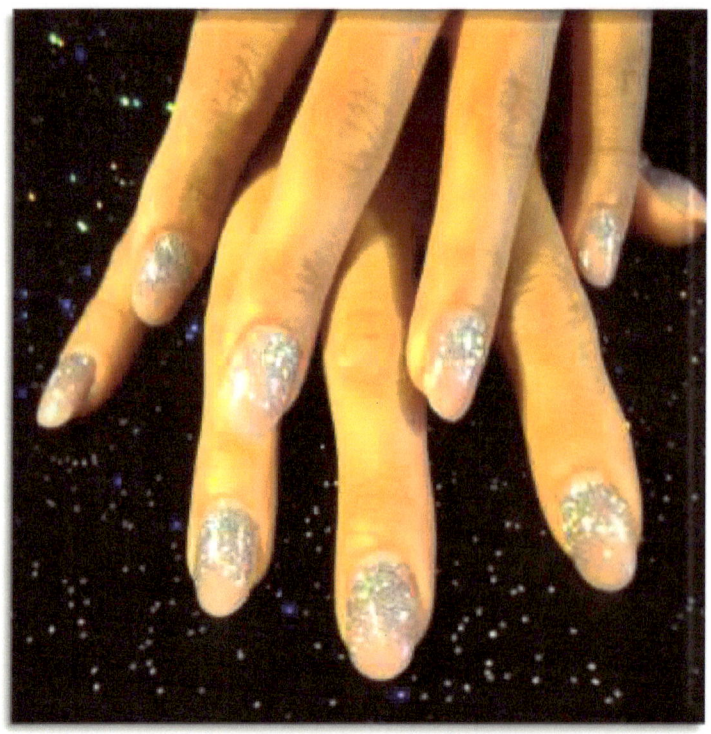

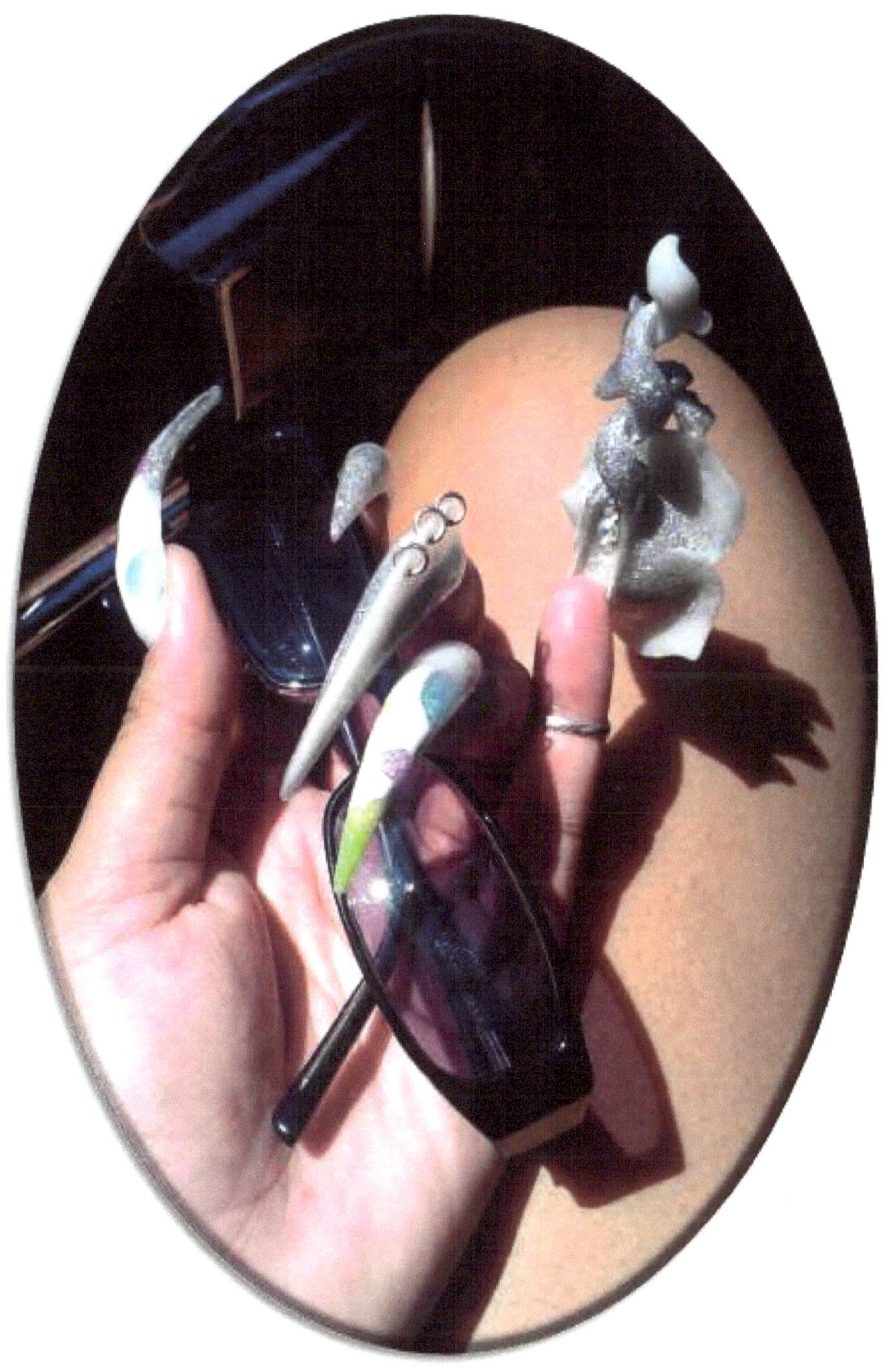

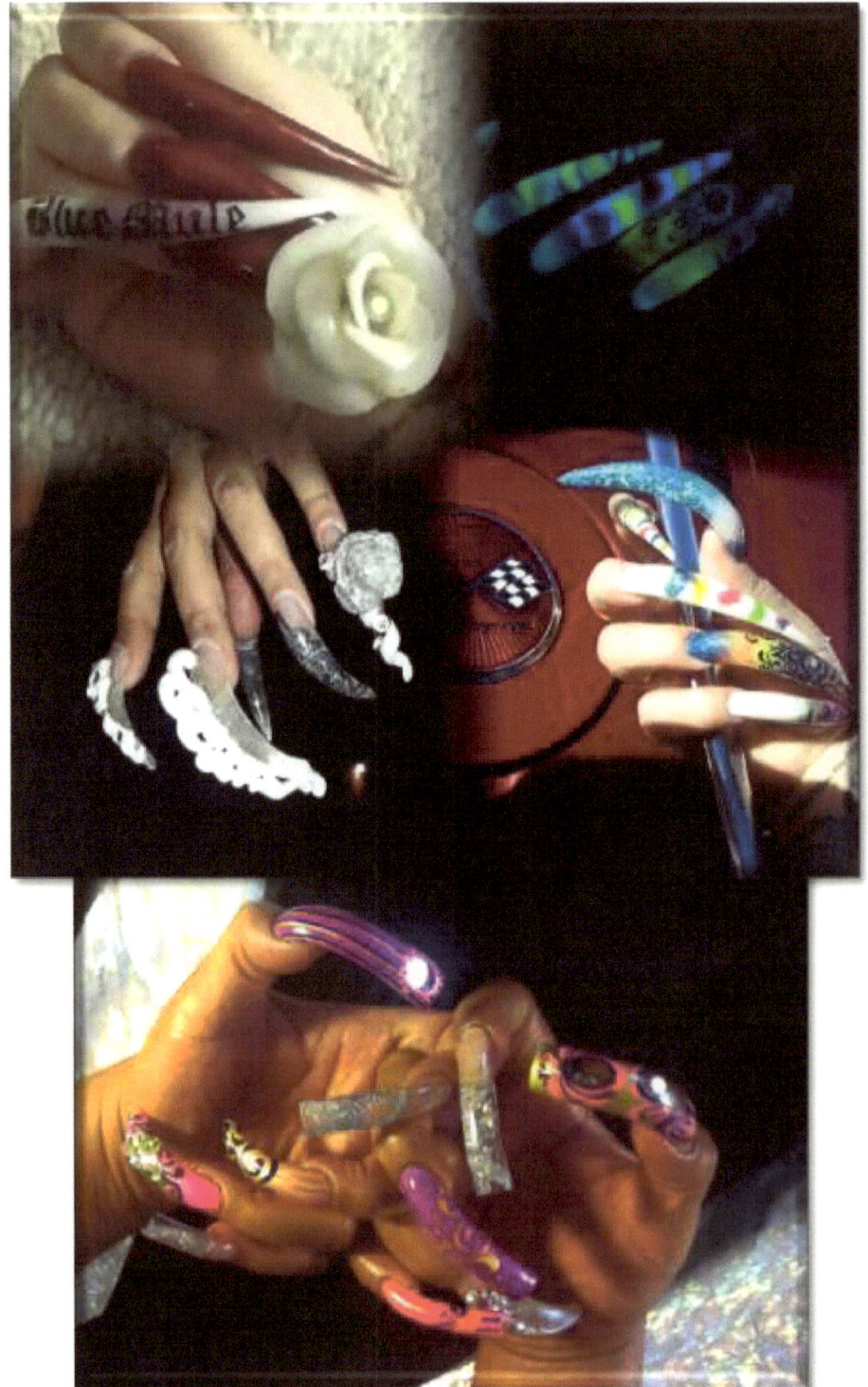

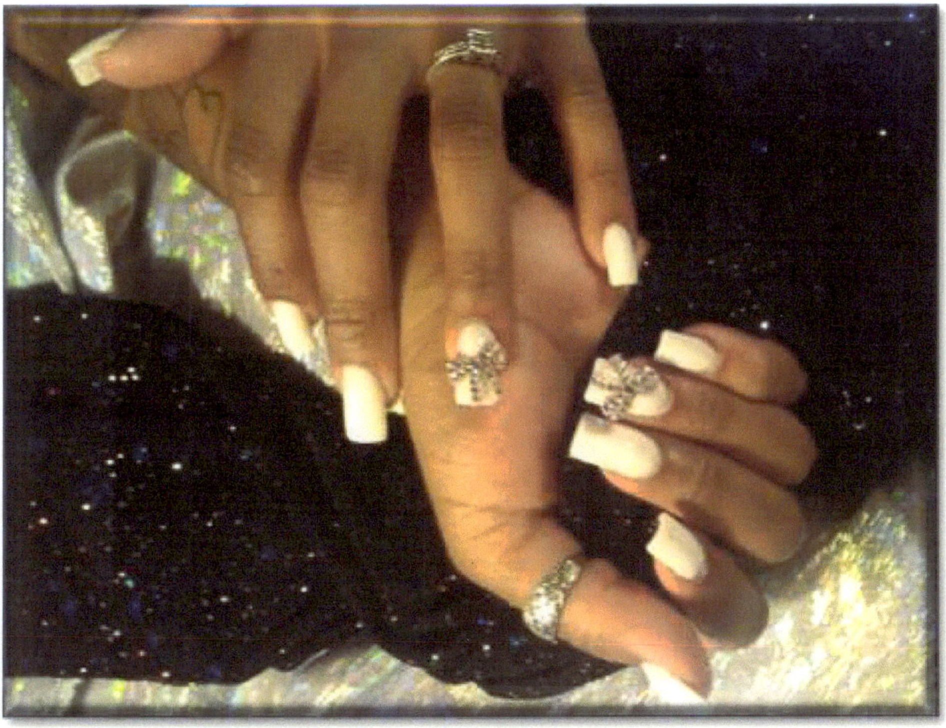

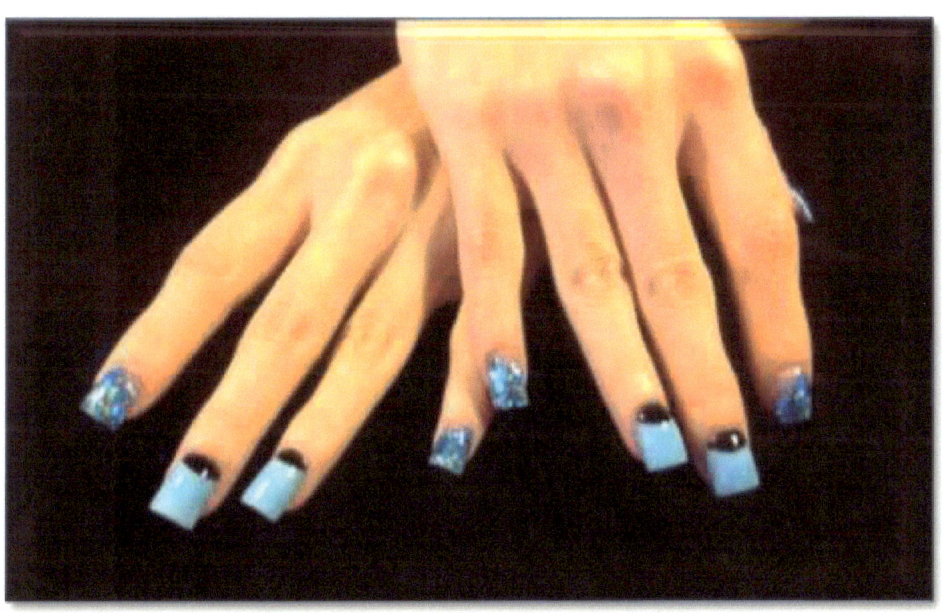

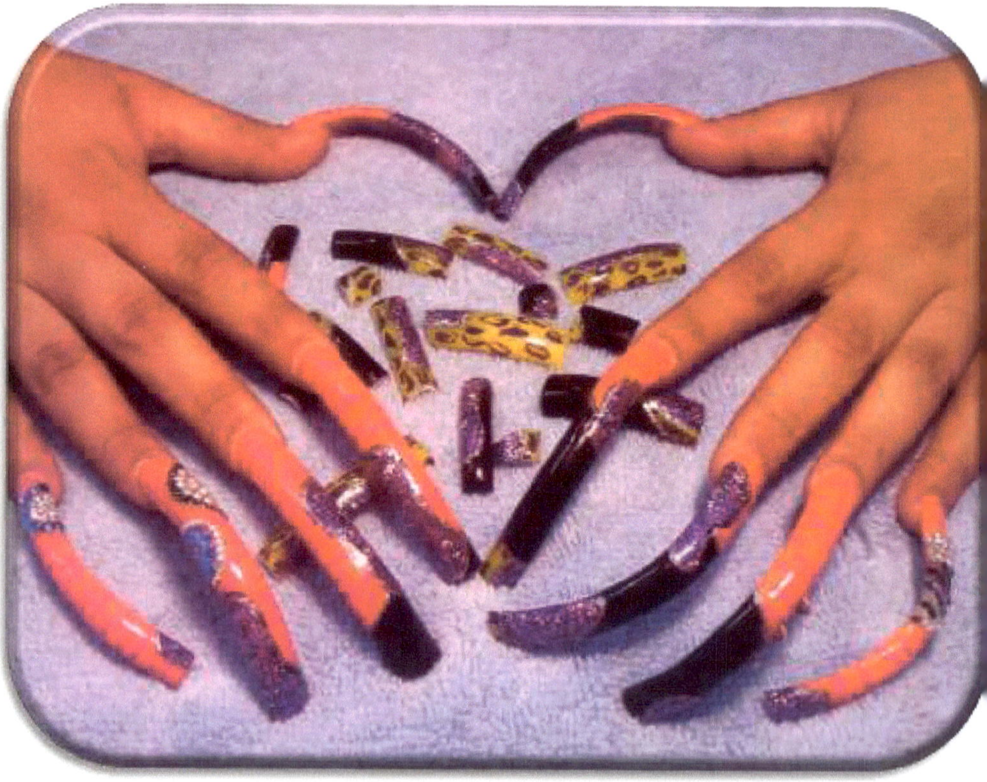

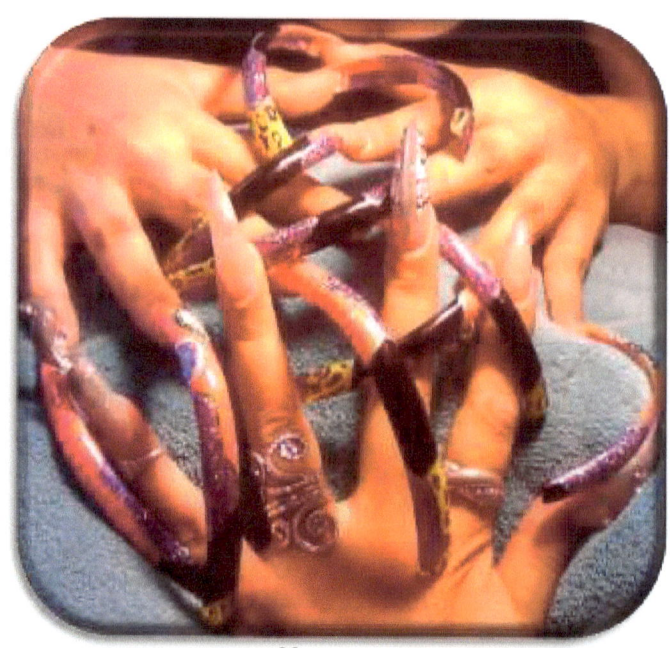

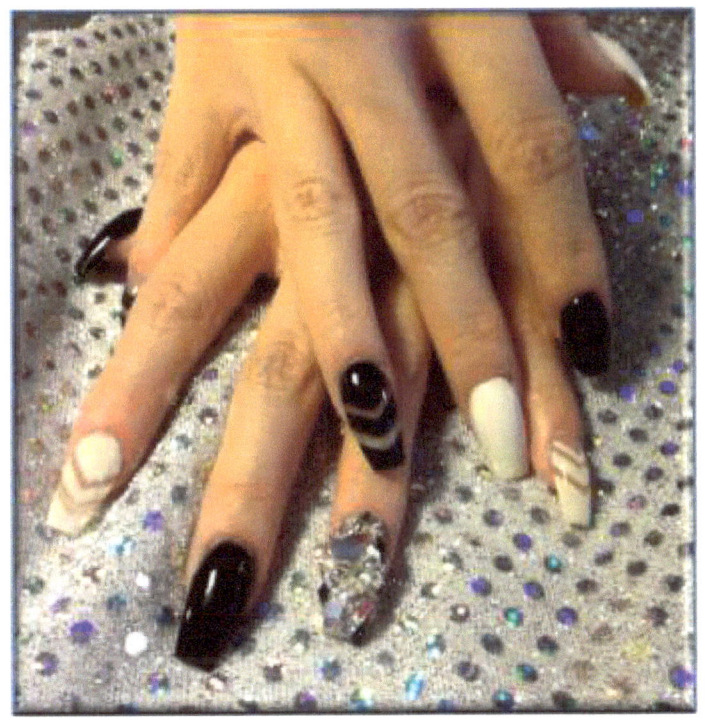

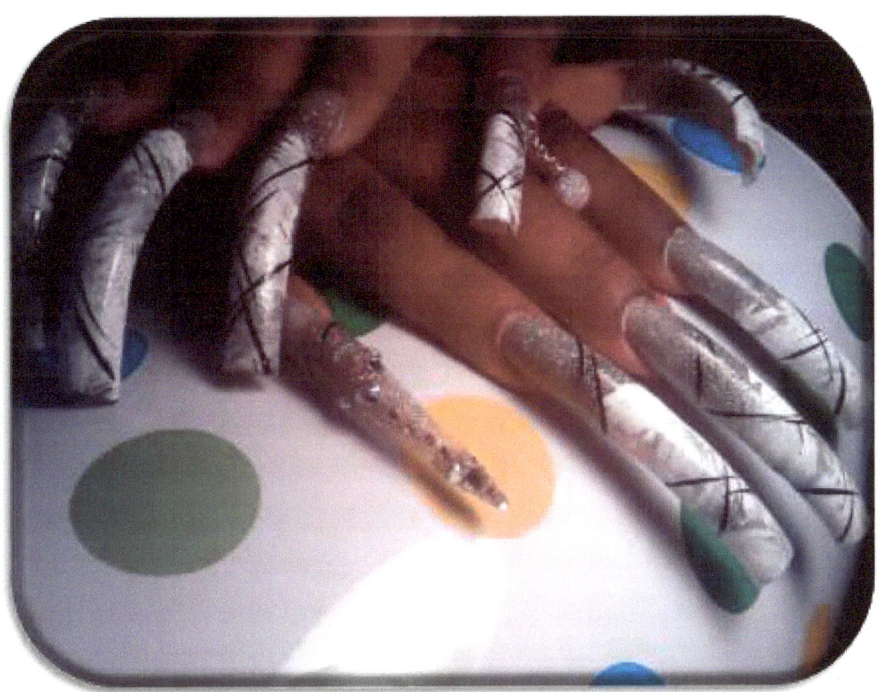

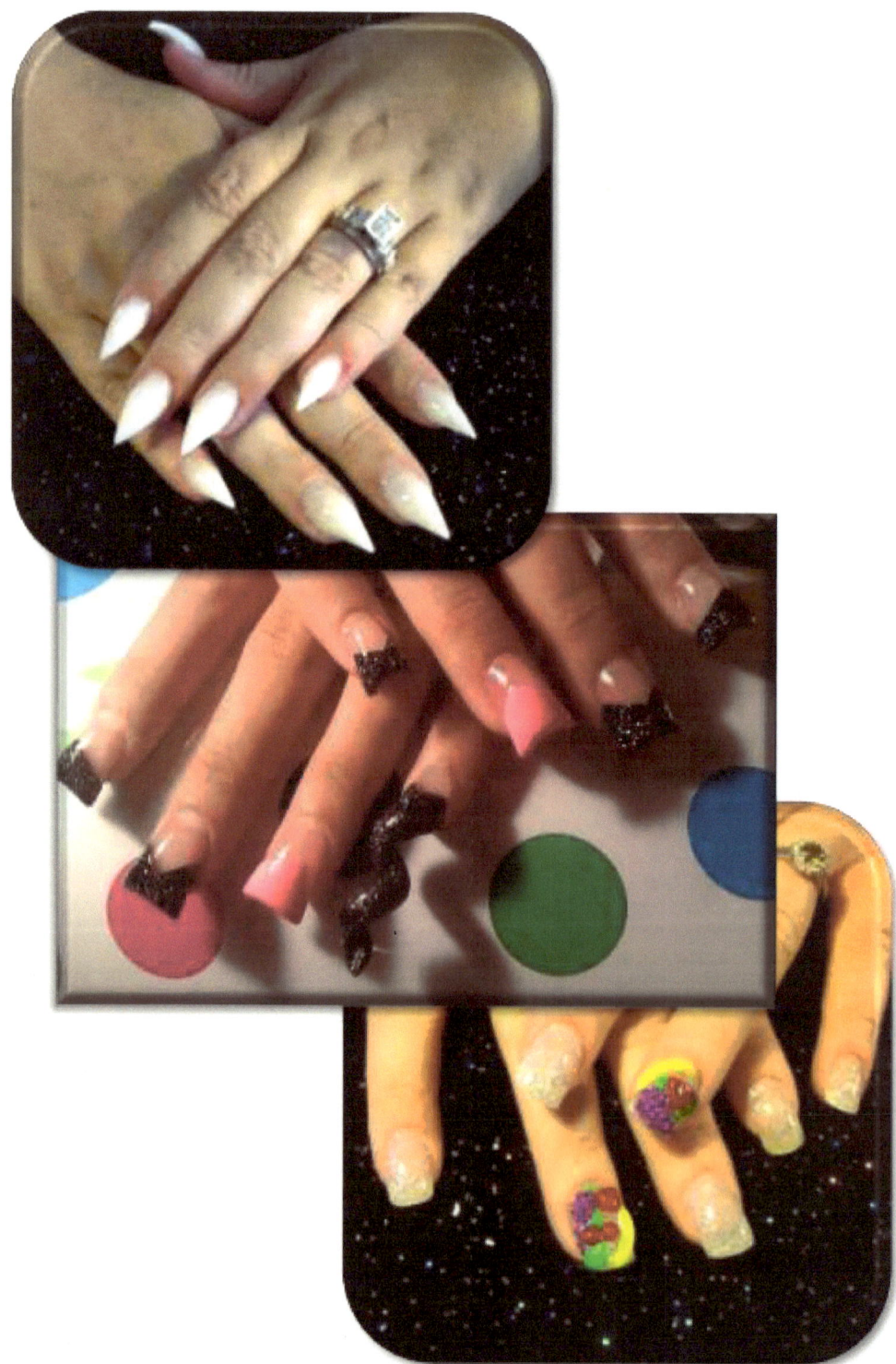

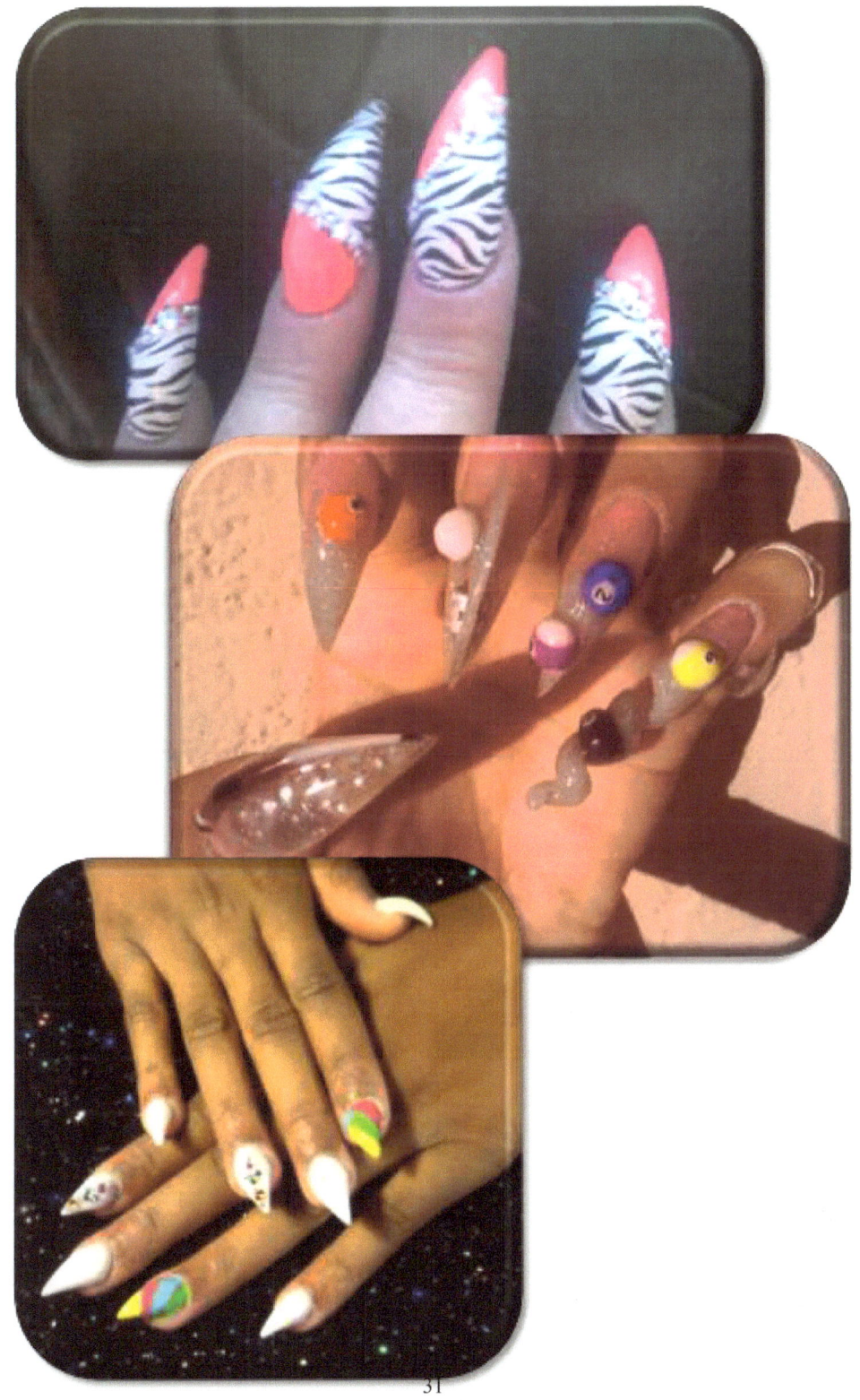

ABOUT The AUThOR

One of my earliest memories in life was me being a little girl hiding in my closet with a bottle of my aunts deep purple nail polish and concentrating really hard to polish the nails on my right hand while using my left hand. Needless to say it was a mess! Gratefully, I have not only developed this talent now but I also do my nails ambidextrously while having a red/green color deficiency. At around 12 years old my adventure in acrylic nails began as my parents encouraged me to explore my own talents. I asked them for a do-it-yourself acrylic nail kit and they provided it. For the next 17 years I would do my own nails practicing the art of shaping a nail, hand painting, custom 3D sculpted design, use of piercings and rhinestones. During my high school years I would use piercings along with nail art decals and multi-colored nail polishes to decorate my nails. Over the years many people suggested that I pursue a career with my talents surrounding nails and after many life changes I became a licensed manicurist in Las Vegas, NV. I quickly went to work sharing the style of artistry that I had developed over the years with a community of acrylic nail clients who were starved for original customized nail art. During my research I was unable to find a single manicurist offering 3 dimensional, crystal or encapsulated designs in Las Vegas. It may have taken a few years for the community to accept this new "extreme" form of nail art, but slowly the evidence presented itself that it is being appreciated more and more daily. Seeking to create an environment conducive to relaxation, happiness and creativity for my multi-ethnic clientele, I moved on to open Nail Fanatics Artistry Design Studio©2007 on January 1, 2009 where I continue to influence the modern movement of Nail Fanatics©2007 through creativity and talents that I received at birth and developed by choice.

There are no instructions in this book of nail art because I firmly believe that a true artist will be able to find their own inspiration simply by seeing something different. Just as I was inspired we all are open to inspiration, we all have talent. Each artist has their own style and will not come to excel until they develop their own style. My reward comes from seeing the smiles and happiness when clients return to me with stories of different ways that wearing my artwork on the canvas of

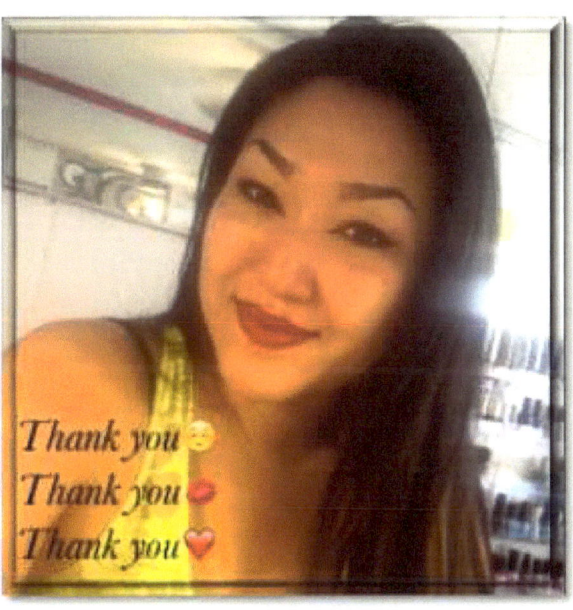

their nails has improved their days. We Nail Fanatics©2007 embrace the giving of compliments and treasure each one shared with us. I offer something positive in this world to all I come in contact with and I have seen artwork do the same thing. Life is hard enough on its own. We don't have to make it harder on each other and although I am "only" doing nails, I know that by the nails I do and the life I live, I inspire others to increase the peace and happiness in their surroundings as well. I am happy to share some of my artwork with you for your pleasure and inspiration. Sending all my readers peace, love and happiness. Thank you. Thank you! Thank YOU!!!

All inquires:

Nail Fanatics Artistry Design Studio
310 E. Lake Mead Boulevard South,   Suite H
North Las Vegas, NV 89030
702.769.3136
NailFanatics@hotmail.com

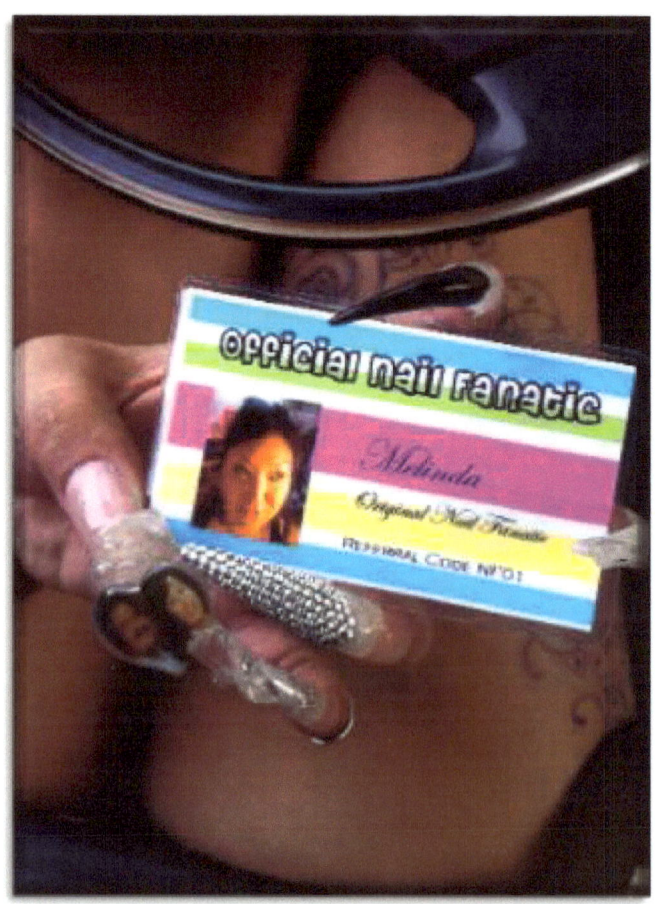

Instagram/Twitter: @nailFADS
Facebook: Nail Fanatics Artistry Design Studio

www.ingramcontent.com/pod-product-compliance
Lightning Source LLC
Chambersburg PA
CBHW041116180526
45172CB00001B/273